The Isms: Modern Doctrines and Movements

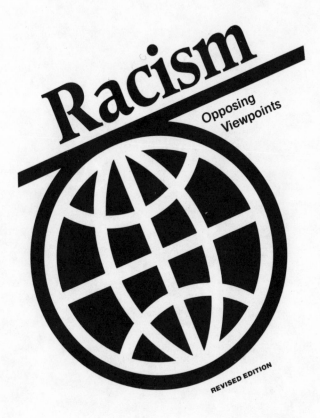

Racism

Opposing Viewpoints

REVISED EDITION

Other Volumes Available in the *ISMS SERIES:*

Capitalism
Communism
Feminism
Internationalism
Nationalism
Socialism

The Isms: Modern Doctrines and Movements

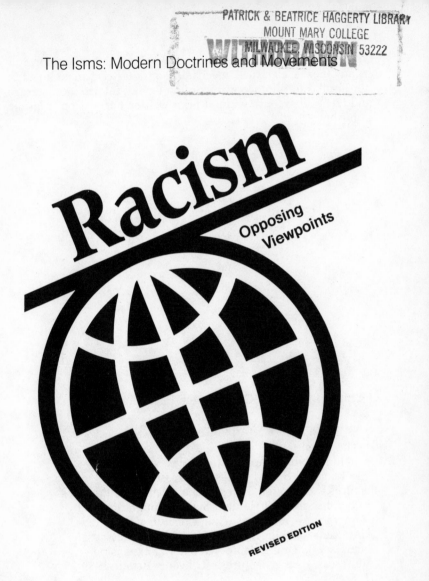

Racism

Opposing
Viewpoints

REVISED EDITION

Bruno Leone

Greenhaven Press
577 Shoreview Park Road
St. Paul, Minnesota 55126

Library of Congress Cataloging-in-Publication Data

Racism : opposing viewpoints.

(The Isms)
Includes bibliographies and index.
1. Racism—United States—Addresses, essays, lectures. 2. United States—Race relations—Addresses, essays, lectures. 3. United States—Emigration and immigration—Addresses, essays, lectures. 4. Afro-Americans—Intelligence levels—Addresses, essays, lectures. 5. United States—Territorial expansion—Addresses, essays, lectures. I. Leone, Bruno, 1939-
II. Series.
E184.A1R33 1986   305.8'00973   86-360
ISBN 0-89908-382-X (lib. bdg.)
ISBN 0-89908-357-9 (pbk.)

Second Edition
Revised

"Congress shall make no law . . . abridging the freedom of speech, or of the press."

first amendment to the U.S. Constitution

The basic foundation of our democracy is the first amendment guarantee of freedom of expression. The Opposing Viewpoints books are dedicated to the concept of this basic freedom and the idea that it is more important to practice it than to enshrine it.

Contents

Chapter 3: Is IQ Testing Racist?

Chapter 4: Is Racial Discrimination Prevalent?

Chapter 5: The Nature of Racism

Why Consider Opposing Viewpoints?

"It is better to debate a question without settling it than to settle a question without debating it."

Joseph Joubert (1754-1824)

The Importance of Examining Opposing Viewpoints

The purpose of the Opposing Viewpoints books, and this book in particular, is to present balanced, and often difficult to find, opposing points of view on complex and sensitive issues.

Probably the best way to become informed is to analyze the positions of those who are regarded as experts and well studied on issues. It is important to consider every variety of opinion in an attempt to determine the truth. Opinions from the mainstream of society should be examined. But also important are opinions that are considered radical, reactionary, or minority as well as those stigmatized by some other uncomplimentary label. An important lesson of history is the eventual acceptance of many unpopular and even despised opinions. The ideas of Socrates, Jesus, and Galileo are good examples of this.

Readers will approach this book with their own opinions on the issues debated within it. However, to have a good grasp of one's own viewpoint, it is necessary to understand the arguments of those with whom one disagrees. It can be said that those who do not completely understand their adversary's point of view do not fully understand their own.

A persuasive case for considering opposing viewpoints has been presented by John Stuart Mill in his work *On Liberty*. When examining controversial issues it may be helpful to reflect on this suggestion:

> The only way in which a human being can make some approach to knowing the whole of a subject, is by hearing what can be said about it by persons of every variety of opinion, and studying all modes in which it can be looked at by every character of mind. No wise man ever acquired his wisdom in any mode but this.

Analyzing Sources of Information

The Opposing Viewpoints books include diverse materials taken from magazines, journals, books, and newspapers, as well as statements and position papers from a wide range of individuals, organizations and governments. This broad spectrum of sources helps to develop patterns of thinking which are open to the consideration of a variety of opinions.

Pitfalls to Avoid

A pitfall to avoid in considering opposing points of view is that of regarding one's own opinion as being common sense and the most rational stance and the point of view of others as being only opinion and naturally wrong. It may be that another's opinion is correct and one's own is in error.

Another pitfall to avoid is that of closing one's mind to the opinions of those with whom one disagrees. The best way to approach a dialogue is to make one's primary purpose that of understanding the mind and arguments of the other person and not that of enlightening him or her with one's own solutions. More can be learned by listening than speaking.

It is my hope that after reading this book the reader will have a deeper understanding of the issues debated and will appreciate the complexity of even seemingly simple issues on which good and honest people disagree. This awareness is particularly important in a democratic society such as ours where people enter into public debate to determine the common good. Those with whom one disagrees should not necessarily be regarded as enemies, but perhaps simply as people who suggest different paths to a common goal.

Developing Basic Reading and Thinking Skills

In this book carefully edited opposing viewpoints are purposely placed back to back to create a running debate; each viewpoint is preceded by a short quotation that best expresses the author's main argument. This format instantly plunges the reader into the midst of a controversial issue and greatly aids that reader in mastering the basic skill of recognizing an author's point of view.

A number of basic skills for critical thinking are practiced in the activities that appear throughout the books in the series. Some of the skills are:

Evaluating Sources of Information The ability to choose from among alternative sources the most reliable and accurate source in relation to a given subject.

Separating Fact from Opinion The ability to make the basic distinction between factual statements (those that can be demonstrated or verified empirically) and statements of opinion (those that are beliefs or attitudes that cannot be proved).

Identifying Stereotypes The ability to identify oversimplified, exaggerated descriptions (favorable or unfavorable) about people and insulting statements about racial, religious or national groups, based upon misinformation or lack of information.

Recognizing Ethnocentrism The ability to recognize attitudes or opinions that express the view that one's own race, culture, or group is inherently superior, or those attitudes that judge another culture or group in terms of one's own.

It is important to consider opposing viewpoints and equally important to be able to critically analyze those viewpoints. The activities in this book are designed to help the reader master these thinking skills. Statements are taken from the book's viewpoints and the reader is asked to analyze them. This technique aids the reader in developing skills that not only can be applied to the viewpoints in this book, but also to situations where opinionated spokespersons comment on controversial issues. Although the activities are helpful to the solitary reader, they are most useful when the reader can benefit from the interaction of group discussion.

Using this book and others in the series should help readers develop basic reading and thinking skills. These skills should improve the readers' ability to understand what they read. Readers should be better able to separate fact from opinion, substance from rhetoric and become better consumers of information in our media-centered culture.

This volume of the Opposing Viewpoints books does not advocate a particular point of view. Quite the contrary! The very nature of the book leaves it to the reader to formulate the opinions he or she finds most suitable. My purpose as publisher is to see that this is made possible by offering a wide range of viewpoints which are fairly presented.

David L. Bender
Publisher

Preface to First Edition

In his book, *The Inequality of Human Races,* Joseph Arthur comte de Gobineau, made the following assertion: *[History] shows us that all civilizations derive from the white race, that none can exist without its help, and that a society is great and brilliant only so far as it preserves the blood of the noble group that created it, provided that this group itself belongs to the most illustrious branch of our species.*

Significantly, de Gobineau's "white race" did not include all who were apparently white. Rather, it specifically encompassed the tall, light-complected, fair-haired, blue-eyed European types whom he called Aryans. He believed that the Alpine and Mediterranean Europeans who, for the most part, inhabited southern and eastern Europe, were beyond the pale of white civilization. Racially, they were the offspring of a series of unholy unions between whites, blacks and yellows. In a word, de Gobineau considered them to be mongrels. For his totally unsubstantiated claim of Aryan superiority, Joseph Arthur comte de Gobineau, has been labeled the "Father of Modern Racism."

Racism is the belief in the inherent superiority of a particular race. It denies the basic equality of humankind and correlates ability with biological endowment. Thus, it assumes that success or failure in any societal endeavor will depend upon genetic composition rather than environmental advantage.

Since racism itself is ideologically and scientifically indefensible, its principal danger resides in the fact that people and nations often have translated the belief into public policy. Wholesale discrimination, either by fact or by law, has often resulted in the virtual isolation of a specific group or groups from the political, social and economic mainstream of a nation's life. Under more ominous circumstances, the elimination of the "inferior" race has been the rule. The Holocaust in Nazi Germany was Hitler's brand of racism carried to the extreme.

Although this book focuses upon racism in America, it is crucial to realize that racism is not solely an American phenomenon. Peoples of many nations, of differing colors and at various times in history, have been and continue to be equally culpable.

Preface to
Second Edition

It is with pleasure and an enormous degree of satisfaction that the second edition of Greenhaven Press's *ISMS Series: Opposing Viewpoints* has been published. The Series was so well received when it initially was made available in 1978 that plans for its revision were almost immediately formulated. During the following years, the enthusiasm of librarians and classroom teachers provided the editor with the necessary encouragement to complete the project.

While the Opposing Viewpoints format of the series has remained the same, each of the books has undergone a major revision. Because the series is developed along historical lines, materials were added or deleted in the opening chapters only where historical interpretations have changed or new sources were uncovered. The final chapters of each book have been comprehensively recast to reflect changes in the national and international situations since the original titles were published.

The Series began with six titles: *Capitalism, Communism, Internationalism, Nationalism, Racism,* and *Socialism.* A new and long overdue title, *Feminism,* has been added and several additional ones are being considered for the future. The editor offers his deepest gratitude to the dedicated and talented editorial staff of Greenhaven Press for its countless and invaluable contributions. A special thanks goes to Bonnie Szumski, whose gentle encouragement and indomitable aplomb helped carry the developing manuscripts over many inevitable obstacles. Finally, the editor thanks all future readers and hopes that the 1986 edition of the *ISMS Series* will enjoy the same reception as its predecessor.

Were America's Colonial Policies Racist?

Introduction

During the eighteenth and nineteenth centuries, the great European powers, led by England, began to create colonial empires throughout the world. With little regard for the human rights of their native inhabitants, Africa, Asia, and the Indies were methodically colonized in this "scramble" for empire. Where "peaceful" annexation proved impossible, force of arms was utilized as a ready alternative.

By the end of the nineteenth century, the United States was taking a decided stride toward becoming a world power. The carnage and aftermath of the Civil War were fading to bitter memories. America's seemingly endless reserves of natural resources were underwriting adolescent industries which promised to one day dwarf those of world-leading Germany and England. The growing native population and an ever-increasing flow of immigrants from Europe ensured the presence of a work force necessary to staff those industries.

For many political leaders and influential citizens, one thing remained before America could proudly assume its new role in the family of western nations—the acquisition of colonies. The economic and military advantages of a colonial empire were obvious. Colonies provided a ready market for the sale and distribution of surplus goods produced in the mother country. Many were rich in valuable resources which were unavailable at home. Finally, they could serve as naval bases in the event of war and as stepping-stones from which further colonization would be possible.

The defeat of Spain in the Spanish-American War was the opportunity for which the imperialists in the United States had been waiting. The war had begun as a noble effort to free Cuba from the tyranny of Spanish rule; however, with the destruction of the Spanish fleet in the Philippines, it ended as an effort to acquire colonies.

As the following viewpoints illustrate, one of the more frequent justifications for an imperialistic adventure in the Philippines and elsewhere was racist in nature. Claims regarding the intellectual

18

and political superiority of the Anglo-Saxon race as compared to the native "darkies" were abundant and extravagant. As an additional inducement, the well-worn dictums of "Manifest Destiny" and "Divine Mission" were offered should the racial claims seem inadequate.

Anti-imperialist opposition was essentially political in nature. The viewpoint by Carl Schurz is typical of the counter opinion. Schurz noted that colonization by force would seriously undermine the philosophical foundations of American government and might ultimately lead to a corrosion of the democratic ideal.

Significantly, the anti-imperialist forces did not oppose American imperialism on the lofty principle of universal equality. Occasionally, a reference might be made to Henry Clay's contention that God never would have created a race incapable of self-government. Such arguments, however, were rare. It was a time in American history when appeals to the ethical sensibilities of the nation were of small consequence against the weightier arguments of national wealth and international status.

"[God] has made us the master organizers of the world to establish system where chaos reigns."

America Must Colonize

Albert J. Beveridge

Albert Jeremiah Beveridge (1862-1927) was a lawyer, US senator, and historian. A chauvinistic nationalist, he once said: "America first—not only America first, but America only!" He authored *The Russian Advance* (1903), *The Young Man and the World* (1906), and *Meaning of the Times* (1907). In the following viewpoint, Senator Beveridge argues before his senate colleagues that America must not be hesitant in annexing the Philippines. He passionately explains that not only do the nation's best interests demand it, but also God.

As you read, consider the following questions:

1. How does Senator Beveridge describe the American mission?
2. What arguments does he give for making the Philippines an American colony?
3. The author claims that God has been preparing the English-speaking and Teutonic peoples for a major role. What is this role?

From a speech by Senator Albert J. Beveridge on the floor of the US Senate on January 9, 1900.

The times call for candor. The Philippines are ours forever, "territory belonging to the United States," as the Constitution calls them. And just beyond the Philippines are China's illimitable markets. We will not retreat from either. We will not repudiate our duty in the archipelago. We will not abandon our opportunity in the Orient. We will not renounce our part in the mission of our race, trustee, under God, of the civilization of the world. And we will move forward to our work, not howling out regrets like slaves whipped to their burdens, but with gratitude for a task worthy of our strength, and thanksgiving to Almighty God that He has marked us as His chosen people, henceforth to lead in the regeneration of the world.

Philippines Command the Pacific

This island empire is the last land left in all the oceans. If it should prove a mistake to abandon it, the blunder once made would be irretrievable. If it proves a mistake to hold it, the error can be corrected when we will. Every other progressive nation stands ready to relieve us.

But to hold it will be no mistake. Our largest trade henceforth must be with Asia. The Pacific is our ocean. More and more Europe will manufacture the most it needs, secure from its colonies the most it consumes. Where shall we turn for consumers of our surplus? Geography answers the question. China is our natural customer. She is nearer to us than to England, Germany or Russia, the commercial powers of the present and the future. They have moved nearer to China by securing permanent bases on her borders. The Philippines give us a base at the door of all the East.

Lines of navigation from our ports to the Orient and Australia; from the Isthmian Canal to Asia; from all Oriental ports to Australia, converge at and separate from the Philippines. They are a self-supporting, dividend-paying fleet, permanently anchored at a spot selected by the strategy of Providence, commanding the Pacific. And the Pacific is the ocean of the commerce of the future. Most future wars will be conflicts for commerce. The power that rules the Pacific, therefore, is the power that rules the world. And, with the Philippines, that power is and will forever be the American Republic....

Here, then, Senators, is the situation. Two years ago there was no land in all the world which we could occupy for any purpose. Our commerce was daily turning toward the Orient, and geography and trade developments made necessary our commercial empire over the Pacific. And in that ocean we had no commercial, naval, or military base. To-day we have one of the three great ocean possessions of the globe, located at the most commanding commercial, naval, and military points in the eastern seas, within hail of India, shoulder to shoulder with China, richer in its own resources than any equal body of land on the entire globe, and peopled by a race which civilization demands shall be improved. Shall we abandon it? That man little knows the common people of the Republic, little understands the instincts of our race, who thinks we will not hold it fast, and hold it forever, administering just government by simplest methods. We may trick up devices to shift our burden and lessen our opportunity; they will avail us nothing but delay. We may tangle conditions by applying academic arrangements of self-government to a crude situation; their failure will drive us to our duty in the end....

Time for Expansion

Whether they will or no, Americans must now begin to look outward. The growing production of the country demands it. An increasing volume of public sentiment demands it. The position of the United States, between the two Old Worlds and the two great oceans, makes the same claim, which will soon be strengthened by the creation of the new link joining the Atlantic and Pacific. The tendency will be maintained and increased by the growth of the European colonies in the Pacific, by the advancing civilization of Japan, and by the rapid peopling of our Pacific States with men who have all the aggressive spirit of the advanced line of national progress.

Captain Alfred T. Mahan, *The Atlantic Monthly*, 1890.

But, Senators, it would be better to abandon this combined garden and Gibraltar of the Pacific, and count our blood and treasure already spent a profitable loss, than to apply any academic arrangement of self-government to these children. They are not capable of self-government. How could they be? They are not a self-governing race. They are Orientals, Malays, instructed by Spaniards in the latter's worst estate....

A Different Situation

The Declaration of Independence does not forbid us to do our part in the regeneration of the world. If it did, the Declaration would be wrong, just as the Articles of Confederation, drafted by the very same men who signed the Declaration, was found to be wrong. The Declaration has no application to the present situation. It was written by self-governing men for self-governing men....

It was written by men who, for a century and a half, had been experimenting in self-government on this continent, and whose ancestors for hundreds of years before had been gradually developing toward that high and holy estate. The Declaration applies only to people capable of self-government. How dare any man prostitute this expression of the very elect of self-governing peoples to a race of Malay children of barbarism....

Senators in opposition are estopped from denying our constitutional power to govern the Philippines as circumstances may demand, for such power is admitted in the case of Florida, Louisiana, Alaska. How, then, is it denied in the Philippines? Is there a geographical interpretation to the Constitution? Do degrees of longitude fix constitutional limitations? Does a thousand miles of ocean diminish constitutional power more than a thousand miles of land?...

A Colonizing Race

The makers of the Constitution were of the race that produced Hawkins, and Drake, and Raleigh, and Smith, and Winthrop, and Penn. They were of the great exploring, pioneering, colonizing, and governing race who went forth with trade or gain or religious liberty as the immediate occasion for their voyages, but really because they could not help it; because the blood within them commanded them; because their racial tendency is as resistless as the currents of the sea or the process of the suns or any other elemental movement of nature, of which that racial tendency itself is the most majestic. And when they wrote the Constitution they did not mean to negative the most elemental characteristic of their race, of which their own presence in America was an expression and an example. You can not interpret a constitution without understanding the race that wrote it. And if our fathers had intended a reversal of the very nature and being of their race, they would have so declared in the most emphatic words our language holds. But they did not, and in the absence of such words the power would remain which is essential to the strongest tendency of our practical race, to govern wherever we are, and to govern by the methods best adapted to the situation. But our fathers were not content with silence, and they wrote in the Constitution the words which affirm this essential and imperial power.

The Question Is Racial

This question is deeper than any question of party politics; deeper than any question of the isolated policy of our country even; deeper even than any question of constitutional power. It is elemental. It is racial. God has not been preparing the English-speaking and Teutonic peoples for a thousand years for nothing but vain and idle self-contemplation and self-admiration. No! He has made us the master organizers of the world to establish system where chaos reigns. He has given us the spirit of progress to overwhelm the forces of reaction throughout the earth. He has made us adept in government that we may administer government among savage and senile peoples. Were it not for such a force as this the world would relapse into barbarism and night. And of all our race He has marked the American people as His chosen nation to finally lead in the regeneration of the world. This is the divine mission of

23

America, and it holds for us all the profit, all the glory, all the happiness possible to man. We are trustees of the world's progress, guardians of its righteous peace. The judgment of the Master is upon us: "Ye have been faithful over a few things; I will make you ruler over many things."

What shall history say of us? Shall it say that we renounced that holy trust, left the savage to his base condition, the wilderness to the reign of waste, deserted duty, abandoned glory, forgot our sor-

Albert J. Beveridge, senator from Indiana.
United Press International, Inc.

did profit even, because we feared our strength and read the charter of our powers with the doubter's eye and the quibbler's mind? Shall it say that, called by events to captain and command the proudest, ablest, purest race of history in history's noblest work, we declined that great commission? Our fathers would not have had it so. No! They founded no paralytic government, incapable of the simplest acts of administration. They planted no sluggard people, passive while the world's work calls them. They established no reactionary nation. They unfurled no retreating flag....

Blind indeed is he who sees not the hand of God in events so vast, so harmonious, so benign. Reactionary indeed is the mind that perceives not that this vital people is the strongest of the saving forces of the world; that our place, therefore, is at the head of the constructing and redeeming nations of the earth; and that to stand aside while events march on is a surrender of our interests, a betrayal of our duty as blind as it is base. Craven indeed is the heart that fears to perform a work so golden and so noble; that dares not win a glory so immortal.

"No man is good enough to govern another man without the other's consent."

Imperialism Will Ruin America

American Anti-Imperialist League and
Democratic Party

Following the Spanish-American War, a majority of Americans seemed to favor the annexation of the Philippines. Many others, however, were convinced that any imperialistic adventure would ultimately prove fatal to democracy in America. On October 17, 1899, a coalition of anti-imperialist leagues met in Chicago. Calling themselves the American Anti-Imperialist League, they adopted a platform outlining their aims and principles. Part I of the following viewpoint is excerpted from this platform. In 1900, the Democratic party, at its presidential nominating convention, devoted a significant portion of its platform to condemning US imperialism in the Philippines. Part II is excerpted from this platform.

As you read, consider the following questions:

1. How does the Anti-Imperialist League define the policy of the Philippine national administration?
2. What arguments does the League cite for opposing the colonization of the Philippines?
3. What reasons are offered in the Democratic platform for condemning American involvement in the Philippines?

Platform of the American Anti-Imperialist League, October 17, 1899. Platform of the Democratic Party, 1900.

I

We hold that the policy known as imperialism is hostile to liberty and tends toward militarism, an evil from which it has been our glory to be free. We regret that it has become necessary in the land of Washington and Lincoln to reaffirm that all men, of whatever race or color, are entitled to life, liberty and the pursuit of happiness. We maintain that governments derive their just powers from the consent of the governed. We insist that the subjugation of any people is "criminal aggression" and open disloyalty to the distinctive principles of our Government.

We earnestly condemn the policy of the present National Administration in the Philippines. It seeks to extinguish the spirit of 1776 in those islands. We deplore the sacrifice of our soldiers and sailors, whose bravery deserves admiration even in an unjust war. We denounce the slaughter of the Filipinos as a needless horror. We protest against the extension of American sovereignty by Spanish methods.

We demand the immediate cessation of the war against liberty, begun by Spain and continued by us. We urge that Congress be promptly convened to announce to the Filipinos our purpose to concede to them the independence for which they have so long fought and which of right is theirs.

The United States have always protested against the doctrine of international law which permits the subjugation of the weak by the strong. A self-governing state cannot accept sovereignty over an unwilling people. The United States cannot act upon the ancient heresy that might makes right.

A Danger to Democracy

Imperialists assume that with the destruction of self-government in the Philippines by American hands, all opposition here will cease. This is a grievous error. Much as we abhor the war of "criminal aggression" in the Philippines, greatly as we regret that the blood of the Filipinos is on American hands, we more deeply resent the betrayal of American institutions at home. The real firing line is not in the suburbs of Manila. The foe is of our own household. The attempt of 1861 was to divide the country. That of 1899 is to destroy its fundamental principles and noblest ideals.

Whether the ruthless slaughter of the Filipinos shall end next month or next year is but an incident in a contest that must go on until the Declaration of Independence and the Constitution of the United States are rescued from the hands of their betrayers. Those who dispute about standards of value while the foundation of the Republic is undermined will be listened to as little as those who would wrangle about the small economies of the household while the house is on fire. The training of a great people for a century,

THE WHITE MAN'S BURDEN

Justus in the *Minneapolis Star*. Reprinted by permission.

the aspiration for liberty of a vast immigration are forces that will hurl aside those who in the delirium of conquest seek to destroy the character of our institutions.

We deny that the obligation of all citizens to support their Government in times of grave National peril applies to the present situation. If an Administration may with impunity ignore the issues upon which it was chosen, deliberately create a condition of war anywhere on the face of the globe, debauch the civil service for spoils to promote the adventure, organize a truth-suppressing censorship and demand of all citizens a suspension of judgment and their unanimous support while it chooses to continue the fighting, representative government itself is imperiled.

We propose to contribute to the defeat of any person or party that stands for the forcible subjugation of any people. We shall oppose for reelection all who in the White House or in Congress betray American liberty in pursuit of un-American ends. We still hope that both of our great political parties will support and defend the Declaration of Independence in the closing campaign of the century.

We hold, with Abraham Lincoln, that "no man is good enough to govern another man without that other's consent. When the white man governs himself, that is self-government, but when he governs himself and also governs another man, that is more than self-government—that is despotism." Our reliance is in the love of liberty which God has planted in us. Our defense is in the spirit which prizes liberty as the heritage of all men in all lands. Those who deny freedom to others deserve it not for themselves, and under a just God cannot long retain it.

We cordially invite the cooperation of all men and women who remain loyal to the Declaration of Independence and the Constitution of the United States.

II

We condemn and denounce the Philippine policy of the present administration. It has involved the Republic in an unnecessary war, sacrificed the lives of many of our noblest sons, and placed the United States, previously known and applauded throughout the world as the champion of freedom, in the false and un-American position of crushing with military force the efforts of our former allies to achieve liberty and self-government. The Filipinos cannot be citizens without endangering our civilizations; they cannot be subjects without imperiling our form of government; and as we are not willing to surrender our civilization nor to convert the Republic into an empire, we favor an immediate declaration of the nation's purpose to give the Filipinos, first, a stable form of government; second, independence; and third, protection from outside interference, such as has been given for nearly a century to the republics of Central and South America.

The greedy commercialism which dictated the Philippine policy of the Republican administration attempts to justify it with the plea that it will pay; but even this sordid and unworthy plea fails when brought to the test of facts. The war of "criminal aggression" against the Filipinos, entailing an annual expense of many millions, has already cost more than any possible profit that could accrue from the entire Philippine trade for years to come. Furthermore, when trade is extended at the expense of liberty, the price is always too high.

We are not opposed to territorial expansion when it takes in desirable territory which can be erected into States in the Union, and whose people are willing and fit to become American citizens. We favor trade expansion by every peaceful and legitimate means. But we are unalterably opposed to seizing or purchasing distant islands to be governed outside the Constitution, and whose people can never become citizens.

We are in favor of extending the Republic's influence among the nations, but we believe that that influence should be extended not by force and violence, but through the persuasive power of a high and honorable example.

Entangling Alliances

Maintaining, as I do, the tenets of a line of precedents from Washington's day, which proscribe entangling alliances with foreign states, I do not favor a policy of acquisition of new and distant territory or the incorporation of remote interests with our own.

Grover Cleveland, message to Congress, December 8, 1885.

The importance of other questions, now pending before the American people is no wise diminished and the Democratic party takes no backward step from its position on them, but the burning issue of imperialism growing out of the Spanish war involves the very existence of the Republic and the destruction of our free institutions. We regard it as the paramount issue of the campaign.

"Another marked characteristic of the Anglo-Saxon is what may be called an instinct or genius for colonizing."

The Anglo-Saxon Race Should Colonize the World

Josiah Strong

A clergyman, social reformer, and author, Josiah Strong (1847-1916) was one of the most influential Americans of his day. In 1885 he published his most famous work, *Our Country*, which helped buoy him to national prominence. Strong was convinced that the Anglo-Saxon "race" had reached its zenith in the United States and would one day civilize and Christianize the entire world. In the following viewpoint, he explains why he believes that the Anglo-Saxon race is naturally suited for world colonization.

As you read, consider the following questions:

1. According to Josiah Strong, what are the noblest races?
2. How does he describe the Anglo-Saxon race and its future?
3. What does the author say may be God's final solution for the heathen and inferior peoples?

Josiah Strong, *Our Country*, New York: The Baker & Taylor Company, 1891.

Every race which has deeply impressed itself on the human family has been the representative of some great idea—one or more—which has given direction to the nation's life and form to its civilization....The Anglo-Saxon is the representative of two great ideas, which are closely related. One of them is that of civil liberty. Nearly all of the civil liberty of the world is enjoyed by Anglo-Saxons: the English, the British colonists, and the people of the United States....The noblest races have always been lovers of liberty. The love ran strong in early German blood, and has profoundly influenced the institutions of all the branches of the great German family; but it was left for the Anglo-Saxon branch fully to recognize the right of the individual to himself, and formally to declare it the foundation stone of government.

The other great idea of which the Anglo-Saxon is the exponent is that of a pure *spiritual* Christianity. It was no accident that the great reformation of the sixteenth century originated among a Teutonic, rather than a Latin people....

Again, another marked characteristic of the Anglo-Saxon is what may be called an instinct or genius for colonizing. His unequaled energy, his indomitable perseverance, and his personal independence, made him a pioneer. He excels all others in pushing his way into new countries. It was those in whom this tendency was strongest that came to America, and this inherited tendency has been further developed by the westward sweep of successive generations across the continent. So noticeable has this characteristic become that English visitors remark it. Charles Dickens once said that the typical American would hesitate to enter heaven unless assured that he could go farther west.

Again, nothing more manifestly distinguishes the Anglo-Saxon than his intense and persistent energy, and he is developing in the United States an energy which, in eager activity and effectiveness, is peculiarly American....

The Future of the Anglo-Saxon Race

What is the significance of such facts? These tendencies infold the future; they are the mighty alphabet with which God writes his prophecies. May we not, by a careful laying together of the letters, spell out something of his meaning? It seems to me that God, with infinite wisdom and skill, is training the Anglo-Saxon race for an hour sure to come in the world's future. Heretofore there has always been in the history of the world a comparatively unoccupied land westward, into which the crowded countries of the East have poured their surplus populations. But the widening waves of migration, which millenniums ago rolled east and west from the valley of the Euphrates, meet to-day on our Pacific coast. There are no more new worlds. The unoccupied arable lands of the earth are limited, and will soon be taken. The time is coming when the pressure of population on the means of subsistence will be felt here as it is now felt in Europe and Asia. Then will the world enter upon a new stage of its history—*the final competition of races, for which the Anglo-Saxon is being schooled.* Long before the thousand millions are here, the mighty *centrifugal* tendency, inherent in this stock and strengthened in the United States, will assert itself. Then this race of unequaled energy, with all the majesty of numbers and the might of wealth behind it—the representative, let us hope, of the largest liberty, purest christianity, the highest civilization—having developed peculiarly aggressive traits calculated to impress its institutions upon mankind, will spread itself over the earth. If I read not amiss, this powerful race will move down upon Mexico, down upon Central and South America, out upon the islands of the sea, over upon Africa and beyond. And can any one doubt that the result of this competition of races will be the "survival of the fittest?"

The White Man's Burden

Take up the White Man's burden—
Send forth the best ye breed—
Go bind your sons to exile
To serve your captives' need;
To wait in heavy harness,
On fluttered folk and wild—
Your new-caught, sullen peoples,
Half-devil and half-child....

Take up the White Man's burden—
The savage wars of peace—
Fill full the mouth of Famine
And bid the sickness cease,
And when your goal is nearest
The end for others sought
Watch sloth and heathen Folly
Bring all your hopes to nought....

Rudyard Kipling, "The White Man's Burden."

"Any people," says Dr. Bushnell, "that is physiologically advanced in culture, though it be only in a degree beyond another which is mingled with it on strictly equal terms, is sure to live down and finally live out its inferior. Nothing can save the inferior race but a ready and pliant assimilation. Whether the feebler and more abject races are going to be regenerated and raised up, is already very much of a question. What if it should be God's plan to people the world with better and finer material?...

Whether the extinction of inferior races before the advancing Anglo-Saxon seems to the reader sad or otherwise, it certainly appears probable. I know of nothing except climatic conditions to prevent this race from populating Africa as it has peopled North America. And those portions of Africa which are unfavorable to Anglo-Saxon life are less extensive than was once supposed. The Dutch Boers, after two centuries of life there, are as hardy as any race on earth. The Anglo-Saxon has established himself in climates totally diverse—Canada, South Africa, and India—and, through several generations, has preserved his essential race characteristics. He is not, of course, superior to climatic influences; but even in warm climates, he is likely to retain his aggressive vigor long enough to supplant races already enfeebled. Thus, in what Dr. Bushnell calls "the out-populating power of the Christian stock," may be found God's final and complete solution of the dark problem of heathenism among many inferior peoples....

United States: Gibraltar of the Ages

In my own mind, there is no doubt that the Anglo-Saxon is to exercise the commanding influence in the world's future, but the exact nature of that influence is, as yet, undetermined. How far his civilization will be materialistic and atheistic, and how long it will take thoroughly to Christianize and sweeten it, how rapidly he will hasten the coming of the kingdom wherein dwelleth righteousness, or how many ages he may retard it, is still uncertain; but *is now being swiftly determined.* Let us weld together in a chain the various links of our logic which we have endeavored to forge. Is it manifest that the Anglo-Saxon holds in his hands the destinies of mankind for ages to come? Is it evident that the United States is to be the home of this race, the principal seat of his power, the great center of his influence?...

Notwithstanding the great perils which threaten it, I cannot think our civilization will perish; but I believe it is fully in the hands of the Christians of the United States, during the next ten or fifteen years, to hasten or retard the coming of Christ's kingdom in the world by hundreds, and perhaps thousands, of years. We of this generation and nation occupy the Gibraltar of the ages which commands the world's future.

"The admission as States of the Philippines... would...appear too monstrous to be seriously thought of even by the wildest imperialist."

Colonization Will Destroy Democracy

Carl Schurz

Carl Schurz (1829-1906) emigrated to the United States from Germany in 1852. After obtaining his citizenship, he embarked upon a long and varied career in public service which included minister to Spain, senator from Missouri, and secretary of the interior. He was also the author of a biography of Henry Clay. In the following viewpoint, Senator Schurz claims that America's imperialistic adventure in the Philippines will undermine the very foundation of the nation's democratic traditions.

As you read, consider the following questions:

1. Why does Carl Schurz say the Philippines should never be admitted as states?
2. How would governing distant countries as subject provinces influence our political life at home?
3. How would it influence our future?

Carl Schurz, "Thoughts on American Imperialism," *Century Illustrated*, September 1898.

We are told that as we have grown very rich and very powerful the principles of policy embodied in Washington's Farewell Address have become obsolete; that we have "new responsibilities," "new duties," and a peculiar "mission." When we ask what these new responsibilities and duties require this republic to do, the answer is that it should meddle more than heretofore with the concerns of the outside world for the purpose of "furthering the progress of civilization"; that it must adopt an "imperial policy."...This last proposition has at least the merit of definiteness, and it behooves the American people carefully to examine it in the light of "responsibility," "duty," and "mission."

I am far from denying that this republic, as one of the great powers of the world, has its responsibilities. But what is it responsible for? It is to be held, or to hold itself, responsible for the correction of all wrongs done by strong nations to weak ones, or by powerful oppressors to helpless populations? Is it, in other words, "responsible for the general dispensation of righteousness throughout the world?" [I do not] deny that this republic has a "mission"; and I am willing to accept, what we are frequently told that this mission consists in "furthering the progress of civilization." But does this mean that wherever obstacles to the progress of civilization appear, this republic should at once step in to remove those obstacles by means of force, if friendly persuasion does not avail? Every sober-minded person will admit that under so tremendous a task any earthly power, however great, would soon break down....

Government Without Consent

The admission as States of the Philippines, the Carolinas, and so on,—that is, the transformation of "the United States of America" into "The United States of America and Asia,"—would, I suppose, appear too monstrous to be seriously thought of even by the wildest imperialist. Those countries, with an aggregate of about ten million inhabitants, would have to be governed as subject provinces, with no expectation of their becoming self-governing States. This means government without the consent of the governed. It means taxation without representation. It means the very things against which the Declaration of Independence remonstrated, and against which the fathers rose in revolution. It means that the American people would carry on over large subject populations a kind of rule against which their own government is the most solemn protest. It may be said that those countries and populations cannot be governed in any other way; but is not that the most conclusive reason why this republic should not attempt to govern them at all?

Against such an attempt there are other reasons hardly less vital. No candid observer of current events in this republic will deny that the exercise of more or less arbitrary rule over distant countries will be apt to produce most pernicious effects upon our public morals.

"A Defender of Liberty and A Friend of Human Rights." From the Carl Schurz monument, Riverside Drive, New York City.

The farther away those subject countries are from close public observation, the richer and more tempting their natural resources, the more unfit their populations for self-government, and the more pronounced the race antagonisms, the more unrestrained will be the cupidity of the governing race, the less respect will there be for the rights and interests of the subject races, and the more unscrupulous and rapacious the rule over them—and this in spite of laws for their protection which may be fair on their face and well intended in their meaning. There has been much complaint of the influence wielded in our government by rich and powerful corporations such as the Sugar Trust. The more or less arbitrary control exercised by our government over distant countries with great resources will inevitably stimulate the multiplication of speculative enterprises with much money behind them, subjecting the government in all its branches to constant pressure and manipulation which cannot fail to produce a most baneful effect upon our politics. Of such things we have experience enough to warn us.

Increase in Political Corruption

But the combinations formed for distant adventure will be the most dangerous of all. Never having enough, their greed constantly grasping for more, they will seek to drive this country into new enterprises of conquest. Opportunities will not be lacking when this republic is once in the race for colonial acquisitions in which the European powers are now engaged, and which keeps them incessantly increasing their expensive armaments. And the more such enterprises there are, the greater will be the danger of new wars, with all their demoralizing effects upon our democratic government. It is, therefore, not too much to say—indeed, it is rather stating the fact very mildly—that the governing of distant countries as subject provinces would result in a fearful increase of the elements of profligacy and corruption in our political life....

The Hypocrisy of America

But suppose we are sanguine and call this not a certainty, but only a danger, what reason have the American people for exposing themselves to a danger so awful? We are told that we produce more than this country can consume, and must have foreign markets in which to sell our surplus products. Well, must we own the countries with which we wish to trade? Is not this a notion ludicrously barbarous? And as to more open markets which we want, will it not, when after this war (Spanish-American) we make our final peace arrangements, be easy to stipulate for open ports?...

Meanwhile, by turning the war advertised so loudly as a war of liberation and humanity into a war of conquest, a land-grabbing foray, the American democracy will have lost its honor. It will stand before the world as a self-convicted hypocrite. It will have verified all that has been said in this respect by its detractors....

And what will become, with all this, of the responsibility of the American people for the maintenance of "the government of the people, by the people, for the people," and of our great mission to further the progress of civilization by enhancing the prestige of democratic institutions? It will be only the old tale of a free people seduced by false ambitions and running headlong after riches and luxuries and military glory, and then down the fatal slope into vice, corruption, decay, and disgrace. The tale will be more ignominious and mournful this time, because the opportunities had been more magnificent, the fall more rapid, and the failure more shameful and discouraging than ever before in history....

The Moral Instinct of America

Some of us are old enough to remember the days when "manifest destiny" and "the irresistible decree of Providence" were with similar assurance invoked in behalf of what was called "extending the area of freedom," which then really meant the acquisition of more territory for the multiplication of slave States. The moral instinct and sound sense of the American people then resisted the seductive cry and silenced it, thus proving that it was neither "destiny" nor "Providence," but only a hollow sound. We may hope that the same moral instinct and sound sense will now resist and silence the same cry.

"Fifty years hence under [American] control the Filipinos, who now retain so many savage instincts, will be orderly, law-abiding persons."

America Has a Civilizing Mission

The Spectator

The Spectator was a London weekly published in the 1800s that provided commentary on politics, literature, theology, and art, and whose editorial policy tended to reflect the political opinions of the majority of British people. Great Britian, a colonial power itself, was, at the time, favorably disposed toward the colonial ambitions of its American cousin. In the following viewpoint, the author argues that "civilized" nations like America should act as a civilizing force upon the "less civilized" peoples of the world.

As you read, consider the following questions:

1. Why does the author believe that America will move ahead with plans to colonize the Philippines?
2. Why does the author believe that American colonial ambitions will be beneficial to native peoples?

The Spectator, London, January 14, 1899.

We have no belief whatever in the opposition which is revealing itself in Washington to the annexation of the Philippines....The policy of America when once defined is not likely to be deflected by the resistance of semi-civilised coloured men, who have not a notion of the irresistible strength they are contending against, and one terrible defeat will probably convince the Tagals that their leaders have deceived them. With the American fleet in movement the islanders are split up into minute sections, the cities are all on the coast exposed to the fire of the shipping, and as to guerilla war, why has it never been successful in driving out the Spaniards? The Americans will pacify the dominant caste, the Tagals, as soon as they have organised native regiments; they have already the support of the Papacy, trembling for its great possessions; and the Spaniards left in the islands having elected to join the civilised side, will at once supply any lack of local knowledge. The real contest will be in Washington, and it will not be very fierce there. America has always parties, and Americans let nothing pass without loud speeches, which they often enjoy as other peoples enjoy music— you may see the same phenomenon in Ireland—but the parties on this occasion are not equal. The Democrats have split, "Boss" Croker, who knows his men, having become as violent for expansion as Mr. Cleveland is violent in opposition to it; while the Republicans of New England, who from tradition distrust the new policy, are overwhelmed by the multitudes of the West, who really govern the Union, and who see in expansion chances of unhoped-for adventure, excitement, and gain.

Public Support

In a recent census of newspapers throughout the Union it was found that two-thirds were for a forward policy, and we question, if a popular vote were taken on the single question, whether even that proportion would represent the majority. The orators of the Opposition reveal, indeed, in their speeches an inner consciousness of unpopularity. They do not venture to say frankly that the Treaty of Peace should be rejected and the Philippines surrendered to Spain, nor do they repeat their first argument, that Americans cannot be trusted to civilise half-blood Malays, but fall back upon the abstract rights of man as defined in the Constitution. The only just basis of government, says Senator Hoar, who probably whips his children when they are naughty, is "the consent of the governed." That argument sounds beautiful; but it is hardly likely to convince Americans, who expended a million lives and six hundred millions sterling in compelling the Southerners to accept a government against which they had rebelled; who refuse all political rights to their home-grown Indians, the original proprietors of the soil; and who, after granting the vote to negroes, suffered it to be rendered valueless by terrorism. Just imagine a Louisianian Representative talking about "consent" after reading of the military occupation by which his State, just after its purchase from Napoleon, was reduced to order, or a Floridan Senator familiar with the history of the savage war which suppressed the Seminoles. Are the Americans, perhaps, going to give up Texas or hand over California to the Mexicans with an apology and a few millions in compensation? All that talk ends in words. If Americans can constitutionally govern dark races within the Union without conceding to them political powers, so they can govern them in distant possessions, and the single thing for them to consider is whether in so governing them they are doing good and not evil. We maintain that they are doing good, that the dark races both of Asia and Africa need a century or two of discipline before their full powers can reveal themselves, and that there are races which can enforce this discipline without tyranny and with a perceptible reduction of the great sum of human misery. We believe the Americans to be one of these, and that fifty years hence under their control the Filipinos, who now retain so many savage instincts, will be orderly, law-abiding persons like our own Hindoos, with a taste for acquiring money, and the foible of believing that rhetoric is an admirable substitute alike for thought and action. Like Arabs and Malays, they are born with the literary predispositions; and as they will speak either Spanish or American, their forms of expression are pretty sure to be a little "highfalutin.' "

The Policy of America

The policy of America when once defined is not likely to be deflected by the resistance of semi-civilised coloured men, who have not a notion of the irresistible strength they are contending against.

The Spectator.

We write these arguments because our business is to discuss; but at heart we doubt whether the great movements of humanity are ever much affected by discussion. Nobody, we may safely assert, ever argued the white barbarians into the conquest of the Roman Empire, or the Arabs into the strange outpouring which submerged Western Asia and North Africa, or the Spaniards into that colonisation of South America which even now is only half explained, or Europeans into that mighty stream of emigration which has changed most of the conditions of the world and probably all its future. Most certainly nobody argued the English into the conquest of India, for there are reams of despatches peremptorily forbidding and censuring almost every step in the process. The great races, when the hour of opportunity arrives, expand greatly,—that is all we really know; and what, when the momentum is on them, they have to care about is to see that their action, for which they are only half responsible, benefits the world.

"[The Filipinos] hate our ways. They are hostile to our ideas."

America Does Not Have a Civilizing Mission

William Graham Sumner

William Graham Sumner (1840-1910) was a professor of political and social science at Yale University and an ordained Episcopal minister. A strong supporter of laissez-faire capitalism, he originated the concept of ethnocentrism, a term now commonly used to designate attitudes of superiority about one's own group in comparison to others. In the following viewpoint, Mr. Sumner contends that the missionary zeal that certain "civilized" nations hold regarding the so-called "uncivilized" peoples of the world is vain, unworthy, and ignoble.

As you read, consider the following questions:

1. What does the author write about the British? the French? the Germans? the Russians?
2. Do you agree with the author's arguments? Why?

William Graham Sumner, *War and Other Essays*. New Haven, CT: Yale University Press, 1911. Reprinted with permission.

There is not a civilized nation which does not talk about its civilizing mission just as grandly as we do. The English, who really have more to boast of in this respect than anybody else, talk least about it, but the Phariseeism with which they correct and instruct other people have made them hated all over the globe. The French believe themselves the guardians of the highest and purest culture, and that the eyes of all mankind are fixed on Paris, whence they expect oracles of thought and taste. The Germans regard themselves as charged with a mission, especially to us Americans, to save us from egoism and materialism. The Russians, in their books and newspapers, talk about the civilizing mission of Russia in language that might be translated from some of the finest paragraphs in our imperialistic newspapers. The first principle of Mohammedanism is that we Christians are dogs and infidels, fit only to be enslaved or butchered by Moslems. It is a corollary that wherever Mohammedanism extends it carries, in the belief of its votaries, the highest blessings, and that the whole human race would be enormously elevated if Mohammedanism should supplant Christianity everywhere.

The Hypocrisy of Spain

To come, last, to Spain, the Spaniards have, for centuries, considered themselves the most zealous and self-sacrificing Christians, especially charged by the Almighty, on this account, to spread true religion and civilization over the globe. They think themselves free and noble, leaders in refinement and the sentiments of personal honor, and they despise us as sordid money-grabbers and heretics. I could bring you passages from peninsular authors of the first rank about the grand role of Spain and Portugal in spreading freedom and truth. Now each nation laughs at all the others when it observes these manifestations of national vanity. You may rely upon it that they are all ridiculous by virtue of these pretentions, including ourselves. The point is that each of them repudiates the standards of the others, and the outlying nations, which are to be civilized, hate all the standards of civilized men. We assume that what we like and practice, and what we think better, must come as a welcome blessing to Spanish-Americans and Filippinos. This is grossly and obviously untrue. They hate our ways. They are hostile to our ideas. Our religion, language, institutions, and manners offend them. They like their own ways, and if we appear amongst them as rulers, there will be social discord in all the great departments of social interest. The most important thing which we shall inherit from the Spaniards will be the task of suppressing rebellions. If the United States takes out of the hands of Spain her mission, on the ground that Spain is not executing it well, and if this nation in its turn attempts to be schoolmistress to others, it will shrivel up into the same vanity and self-conceit of which Spain now presents an example. To read our current literature one would think that we were already well on the way to it. Now, the great reason why all these enterprises which begin by saying to somebody else, We know what is good for you better than you know yourself and we are going to make you do it, are false and wrong is that they violate liberty; or, to turn the same statement into other words, the reason why liberty, of which we Americans talk so much, is a good thing is that it means leaving people to live

Conquest Not Pretty

The conquest of the earth, which mostly means the taking it away from those who have a different complexion or slightly flatter nose than ourselves, is not a pretty thing when you look into it.

Joseph Conrad, *Heart of Darkness*, 1902.

out their own lives in their own way, while we do the same. If we believe in liberty, as an American principle, why do we not stand by it? Why are we going to throw it away to enter upon a Spanish policy of dominion and regulation?

Recognizing Stereotypes

A stereotype is an oversimplified or exaggerated discription of people or things. Stereotyping can be favorable. However, most stereotyping tends to be highly uncomplimentary and, at times, degrading.

Stereotyping grows out of our prejudices. When we stereotype someone, we are prejudging him or her. Consider the following example: A Massachusetts college professor has two students from Texas in her class. Both students are late to class every day and do poor work. The professor concludes that all Texans are irresponsible and unintelligent. The next time she has a Texan student in class she singles him out and tells him not to be late to class. The professor is seeing only her stereotype of Texan students, not the student himself.

The following statements relate to the subject matter in this chapter. Consider each statement carefully. *Mark S for any statement that is an example of stereotyping. Mark N for any statement that is not an example of stereotyping. Mark U if you are undecided about any statement.*

If you are doing this activity as a member of a class or group, compare your answers with those of other class or group members. Be able to defend your answers. You may discover that others will come to different conclusions than you. Listening to the reasons others present for their answers may give you valuable insights into recognizing stereotypes.

If you are reading this book alone, ask others if they agree with your answers. You too will find this interaction very valuable.

S = *stereotype*
N = *not a stereotype*
U = *undecided*

1. Orientals are not capable of self-government.

2. The Malays are a race of barbaric children.

3. Asians are invariably intelligent and industrious.

4. All people, of whatever race or color, are entitled to life, liberty and the pursuit of happiness.

5. No one is good enough to govern another person without that person's consent.

6. Nothing more manifestly distinguishes the Anglo-Saxon than his intense and persistent energy.

7. Filipinos live in an impoverished but beautiful country.

8. The English talk grandly about colonization.

9. Every Frenchman believes himself the guardian of the highest and purest culture.

10. The Germans believe they have to save us from egoism and materialism.

11. The Spaniards have for centuries considered themselves the most zealous and self-sacrificing Christians.

12. The religious reformation of the sixteenth century originated among a Teutonic people.

13. The Americans are sordid money-grabbers and heretics.

14. Americans talk too much.

15. America was predominately colonized by white, Anglo-Saxon peoples.

16. The Filipinos are too ignorant to become American citizens.

17. Americans love speeches.

18. In a newspaper census it was found that two-thirds were for colonizing the Philippines.

19. Americans produce more goods than they can consume.

Bibliography

The following list of books, periodicals, and pamphlets deals with the subject matter of this chapter.

Robert L. Beisner — *Twelve Against Empire: The Anti-Imperialists.* New York: McGraw-Hill, 1968.

J.F. Carter — *Conquest: America's Painless Imperialism.* New York: Harcourt Brace and Company, Inc., 1928.

I.M. Destler and Leslie H. Gelb — *The Unmaking of American Foreign Policy.* New York: Simon and Schuster, 1985.

Michael Edwards — *The West in Asia.* New York: Putnam, 1967.

Russell Evans — "The Monroe Doctrine: Still Valid," *Conservative Digest*, April 1985.

Richard Koebner and Helmut von Schmidt — *Imperialism: The Story and Significance of a Word.* Cambridge, England: University Press, 1965.

Walter LaFeber — *The New Empire: An Interpretation of American Expansion 1860-1898.* Ithaca, NY: Cornell University Press, 1963.

George Lichtheim — *Imperialism.* New York: Praeger, 1971.

Nathaniel Peffer — *The White Man's Dilemma: Climax of the Age of Imperialism.* New York: The John Day Company, 1927.

John G. Roberts — *The Colonial Conquest of Asia.* New York: F. Watts, 1976.

Ronald Steel — *Pax Americana.* New York: Penguin, 1970.

W. Scott Thompson — *The Third World: Premises of U.S. Policy.* San Francisco: ICS Press, 1983.

Sanford J. Ungar — *Estrangement: America and the World.* New York: Oxford University Press, 1985.

Rubin F. Weston — *Racism in U.S. Imperialism.* Columbia, SC: University of South Carolina Press, 1972.

Were America's Immigration Policies Racist?

Introduction

The history of America is a history of its immigrants. Since the founding of Virginia by English colonists in 1607, each successive wave of immigrants has made its special contribution to that peculiar amalgam we call American society.

In the colonial period and during the first century of the Republic's history, the overwhelming majority of immigrants came from northern and western Europe. Seeking political and religious freedom and economic opportunities, the English, Scots, Welsh, Irish, Germans, and Scandinavians came to America in unprecedented numbers. The vastness of the western frontier and the rapid growth of industry made possible the ready absorption of these groups into American life.

In addition to the mutual desire to enrich their lives, these early immigrants had other things in common. Virtually all were white and members of the so-called Anglo-Saxon and Nordic races. With the exception of the Irish Catholics and some Germans, all were Protestants. Thus, while language differences often existed, these groups experienced a strong ethnic and religious camaraderie.

The character of American immigration, however, underwent a sudden change near the beginning of the twentieth century. While the white Anglo-Saxon Protestant (WASP) groups continued to immigrate, they did so in smaller numbers. In their place, a new wave of immigrants from southern and eastern Europe found sanctuary in America. This new wave included Italians, Poles, Greeks, Hungarians, Rumanians, and Russians.

Many political leaders and influential Americans considered these newcomers a threat to the American way of life. The new immigrants were not Anglo-Saxon. Moreover, some social and biological scientists did not consider them "white," believing instead that they were racially mixed or "mongrelized." The majority were Catholics, while many, especially the Russians, were Jews. It was felt that these racially different "foreigners" did not possess and could never develop a basic appreciation of America and its sacred institutions. If permitted to enter the United States in large numbers, as they had been doing, they would soon out-

50

number the "native" WASPs, and the future would hold disastrous consequences. Racially, America too would become mongrelized and with it, its institutions.

In response to these fears, American "nativists" began proposing that legal limitations be placed on the numbers of immigrants allowed into the United States. This course of action was not without precedent. In 1902, Congress had suspended indefinitely Chinese immigration. In 1913, the California state legislature, in an attempt to discourage Japanese immigration, had passed the Alien Land Act, barring Japanese from owning land in the state. And, in 1917, Congress overrode two presidential vetoes of a bill requiring mandatory literacy tests for all immigrants.

Immigrants in "steerage" on the S.S. Prince Frederich Wilhelm, July 29, 1915.

United Press International, Inc.

The time for such legislation was especially opportune. Following World War I, an isolationist atmosphere enveloped the nation. The war had dampened America's enthusiasm for things foreign. Moreover, the success of the Bolshevik Revolution in Russia gave rise, in many quarters, to the fear of international communism. This "Red Scare," as it was called in America, was translated into a suspicion of foreigners in general and led to the seizure and deportation of thousands of alien radicals. Finally, a flood of racist literature denigrating the racial and cultural backgrounds of unwanted ethnic groups began saturating bookstores and libraries in the United States. Madison Grant's *The Passing of the Great Race*, which called for the exclusion of "inferior" Alpine, Mediterranean, and Jewish peoples, was typical of these publications.

The finale to this antiforeign drama was played in Washington, DC and written by Congress. On May 19, 1921, a bill was passed limiting the number of immigrants from a given country to three percent of that nationality resident in the United States according to the census of 1910. When further research revealed that the Japanese, Greeks, Hungarians, Italians, Russian Jews, and other "undesirables" had experienced their peak immigration years prior to 1910, additional legislation was planned. The "problem" was ultimately resovled with a new National Origins Quota Act. Passed on May 26, 1924, it limited annual immigration from a given country to two percent of the nationals of that country residing in the United States as of 1890. The bill also provided for the total exclusion of the Japanese.

America's centuries-old policy of virtually unlimited immigration was dramatically reversed. The new law was deliberately weighted to favor the European WASP. One caustic wit felt compelled to suggest that the invitation at the base of the Statue of Liberty be revised to read: "Give me your tired, your poor, your huddled masses yearning to breathe free, but first have them forward their pedigree."

"The native [i.e. white] American will entirely disappear. He will not intermarry with inferior races, and he cannot compete in the sweat shop and in the street trench with the newcomers."

Inferior Races Are Ruining America

Madison Grant

Madison Grant (1865-1937), a graduate of Yale and Columbia Universities, was a lawyer, traveler, hunter, and explorer. He was a trustee of the American Museum of Natural History, president of the New York Zoological Society as well as vice president of the Immigration Restriction League. In the following viewpoint, the author maintains that America's dominant "racial" stock, composed primarily of "white" Nordic and Teutonic peoples, will become diluted beyond recognition by the massive influx of immigrants from Southern and Eastern Europe.

As you read, consider the following questions:

1. According to the author, what was happening to the "native American" by the middle of the nineteenth century?
2. Why does the author believe that the Civil War checked the development and expansion of the "native American"?
3. What reason does the author offer for the decline in the birth rate of "native Americans"?

Madison Grant, *The Passing of the Great Race*. New York: Charles Scribner's Sons, 1916. Reprinted with permission.

Race consciousness in the Colonies and in the United States, down to and including the Mexican War, seems to have been very strongly developed among native Americans, and it still remains in full vigor to-day in the South, where the presence of a large negro population forces this question upon the daily attention of the whites.

In New England, however, whether through the decline of Calvinism or the growth of altruism, there appeared early in the last century a wave of sentimentalism, which at that time took up the cause of the negro, and in so doing apparently destroyed, to a large extent, pride and consciousness of race in the North. The agitation over slavery was inimical to the Nordic race, because it thrust aside all national opposition to the intrusion of hordes of immigrants of inferior racial value, and prevented the fixing of a definite American type....

White Native Americans

The native American by the middle of the nineteenth century was rapidly becoming a distinct type. Derived from the Teutonic part of the British Isles, and being almost purely Nordic, he was on the point of developing physical peculiarities of his own slightly variant from those of his English forefathers....The Civil War, however, put a severe, perhaps fatal, check to the development and expansion of this splendid type, by destroying great numbers of the best breeding stock on both sides, and by breaking up the home ties of many more. If the war had not occurred these same men with their descendants would have populated the Western States instead of the racial nondescripts who are now flocking there.

The prosperity that followed the war attracted hordes of newcomers who were welcomed by the native Americans to operate factories, build railroads, and fill up the waste spaces—"developing the country" it was called.

The New Immigrants

These new immigrants were no longer exclusively members of the Nordic race as were the earlier ones who came of their own impulse to improve their social conditions. The transportation lines advertised America as a land flowing with milk and honey, and the European governments took the opportunity to unload upon careless, wealthy, and hospitable America the sweepings of their jails and asylums. The result was that the new immigration, while it still included many strong elements from the north of Europe, contained a large and increasing number of the weak, the broken, and the mentally crippled of all races drawn from the lowest stratum of the Mediterranean basin and the Balkans, together with hordes of the wretched, submerged populations of the Polish Ghettos.

With a pathetic and fatuous belief in the efficacy of American

54

institutions and environment to reverse or obliterate immemorial hereditary tendencies, these newcomers were welcomed and given a share in our land and prosperity. The American taxed himself to sanitate and educate these poor helots, and as soon as they could speak English, encouraged them to enter into the political life, first of municipalities, and then of the nation.

Disastrous Consequences

The result is showing plainly in the rapid decline in the birth rate of native Americans because the poorer classes of Colonial stock, where they still exist, will not bring children into the world to compete in the labor market with the Slovak, the Italian, the Syrian, and the Jew. The native American is too proud to mix socially with them, and is gradually withdrawing from the scene, abandoning to these aliens the land which he conquered and developed. The man of the old stock is being crowded out of many country districts by these foreigners, just as he is to-day being literally driven off the streets of New York City by the swarms of Polish Jews. These immigrants adopt the language of the native American; they wear his clothes; they steal his name; and they are beginning to take his women, but they seldom adopt his religion or understand his ideals, and while he is being elbowed out of his own home the American looks calmly abroad and urges on others the suicidal ethics which are exterminating his own race.

What Goes in Must Come Out

What goes into the Melting-Pot determines what must come out of it. If we put into it sound, sturdy stock, akin to the pioneer breed which first peopled this country and founded its institutions; if these new stocks are not only sound physically but alert mentally, then we shall develop a race here worthy to carry on the ideals and traditions of the founders of our country. But if the material fed into the Melting-Pot is a polyglot assortment of nationalties, physically, mentally and morally below par, then there can be no hope of producing anything but an inferior race.

Robert DeCourcy Ward, *The Alien in Our Midst*, 1930.

As to what the future mixture will be it is evident that in large sections of the country the native American will entirely disappear. He will not intermarry with inferior races, and he cannot compete in the sweat shop and in the street trench with the newcomers. Large cities from the days of Rome, Alexandria, and Byzantium have always been gathering points of diverse races, but New York is becoming a *cloaca gentium* which will produce many amazing racial hybrids and some ethnic horrors that will be beyond the powers of future anthropologists to unravel.

One thing is certain: in any such mixture, the surviving traits will be determined by competition between the lowest and most primitive elements and the specialized traits of Nordic man; his stature, his light colored eyes, his fair skin and blond hair, his straight nose, and his splendid fighting and moral qualities, will have little part in the resultant mixture.

"When human beings are brought up in an American environment they become Americans, whether their parents were originally Italian, Irish, English, French, German, Japanese, Chinese, or what not."

There Are No Inferior Races

Ashley Montagu

Ashley Montagu is one of the twentieth century's most famous and respected anthropologists. Born in London, England (1905), he immigrated to the United States where he received his Ph.D. in 1937 from Columbia University. During his long and distinguished career, Mr. Montagu has written over three dozen books, many of which deal with the biological and cultural origins of human behavior. In the following viewpoint, the author explains why culture, not genetic makeup, determines the behavioral characteristics of peoples.

As you read, consider the following questions:

1. According to the author, why haven't American Indians acquired the culture of whites?
2. According to the author, why have Australian aboriginals remained so "primitive" in an age of cultural progress?
3. Why does the author believe that "plasticity of mental traits" is of great importance to the human species?

Ashley Montagu, *Statement on Race*. Princeton, NJ: Oxford University Press, 1972. Reprinted with the author's permission.

The question is often asked, "Why is it, since all ethnic groups have had an equal amount of time in which to develop culturally, that there are such great differences between so many of them in cultural development. Surely, the differences are due to innate capacity for development?"

The answer is that time, as such, is a wholly irrelevant factor. Supposing you and I had never been taught to read. Supposing that we live to be a hundred years of age in an illiterate state, can you imagine what our state of cultural development would be like? We should be cut off from almost all those things which make an educated modern man. We would, in short, be illiterates, and the hundred years we had lived would have made very little, if any, difference to our state of illiteracy. Time is irrelevant. What is relevant is the history of our cultural experience.

Culture Determines Behavior

As it is with individuals, so it is with peoples. When human beings are brought up in an American environment they become Americans, whether their parents were originally Italian, Irish, English, French, German, Japanese, Chinese, or what not. By culture they are Americans because they were "culturized" in an American cultural environment, even though they may have been considerably influenced by the cultural heritage of their parents. There are many records of White children who were captured by American Indians and brought up as such who, as adolescents and as adults, were completely indistinguishable from Indians, except, sometimes, in physical appearance, and seldom even then. Similarly White children brought up by Chinese, and American Indian children brought up as Whites, exhibit the cultural traits of the environment in which they were culturally conditioned. Their "ethnic group genes" seem to make no difference whatsoever to their ability to acquire any kind of culture. Furthermore, their ethnic affiliation does not seem ever to express itself in any recognizable elements of the culture or cultures with which their ethnic group may be associated. Ethnic group *cultural* genes simply do not exist. In addition, no ethnic group possesses any genes which set limits upon the acquisition of any culture by any of its members.

The reason why the American Indian has not, on the whole, acquired the culture of the Whites is that he has been segregated from that culture on reservations largely cut off from the main current of American life. As someone once put it, "the trouble with the Red Indian is that he has been tied up with too much red tape."

Similarly, the American Negro has to a large extent been refused admittance to full participation in American culture, and informed that there is no point to his striving to attain any of the desirable places in that culture because these are "for Whites only."

The Australian aboriginal, where he has not been detribalized, is still an Australian aboriginal living in an early Stone Age phase

58

of cultural development, knowing no agriculture or husbandry, having no permanent habitation, and wandering as a nomad over his tribal territory. How is it then that he remains so "primitive" in an age of cultural progress? The answer is that the Australian aboriginal has made a perfectly adequate adaptation to his environment. The fact that he has neither television nor jet planes, nor yet an atom bomb, is due largely to the fact that his own cultural history has been of a sort which has led to the preservation, relatively unaltered, of a way of life fully calculated to meet the needs of a group living by hunting and food gathering in a desert or semi-desert environment. No more and no less....

Importance of Adaptability

Success of the individual in most human societies has depended and continues to depend upon his ability rapidly to evolve behavior patterns which fit him to the kaleidoscope of the conditions he encounters. He is best off if he submits to some, compromises with some, rebels against others, and escapes from still other situations. Individuals who display a relatively greater fixity of response than their fellows suffer under most forms of human society and tend to fall by the way. Suppleness, plasticity, and, most important of all, ability to profit by experience and education are required. No other species is comparable to man in its capacity to acquire new behavior patterns and discard old ones in consequence of training. The survival value of this capacity is manifest, and therefore the possibility of its development through natural selection should be evident.

History Is Proof

History proves that progress in civilization is not the monopoly of one race or subrace. When our forebears in Europe were rude Stone Age primitives, the civilizations of the Babylonians and the Egyptians had already flourished and been eclipsed. There were great Negro states in Africa when Europe was a sparsely settled forest. Negroes made iron tools and wove fine cloth for their clothing when fair-skinned Europeans wore skins and knew nothing of iron.

Ruth Benedict, *Race: Science and Politics*, 1940.

The genetically controlled plasticity of mental traits is, biologically speaking, the most typical and uniquely human characteristic. It is very probable that the survival value of this characteristic in human evolution has been considerable for a long time. Just when this characteristic first appeared is, of course, conjectural. The remains of prehistoric man's cultural activities indicate that the essentially human organization of the mental capacities emerged quite early in the evolution of man. However that may be, the possession of the gene system which conditions educability rather than behavioral fixity, is a common property of all living mankind. In other words, educability is truly a species trait of man, *Homo sapiens,* the animal which, beyond all others, is capable of learning and inventing.

The physical and, even more, the social environments of men who live in different countries are quite diversified. Therefore, it has often been argued, natural selection would be expected to differentiate the human species into local races differing in mental traits. Populations of different countries may differ in skin color, head shape, and other physical traits. Why, then, should they be alike in mental traits?

Why Humans Differ

Arguments based on analogies are precarious, especially where evolutionary patterns are concerned. If human "races" differ in structural traits, it does not necessarily follow that they must also differ in mental ones. "Race" differences arise chiefly because of the differential action of natural selection on geographically separated populations. In the case of man, however, the structural and mental traits are quite likely to be influenced by selection in different ways.

The survival value of a higher development of mental capacities in man is obvious. Furthermore, natural selection seemingly favors such a development everywhere. In the ordinary course of events in almost all societies those persons are likely to be favored who show wisdom, maturity of judgment, and ability to get along with people—qualities which may assume different forms in different cultures. Those are the qualities of the plastic personality, not a single trait but a general condition which appears to have been at a premium in practically all human societies.

Human Flexibility

In human societies, with few exceptions, conditions have been neither rigid nor stable enough to permit the selective breeding of genetic types adapted to different statuses or forms of social organization. Such rigidity and stability do not obtain in any society. On the other hand, the outstanding fact about human societies is that they do change and do so more or less rapidly. The rate of change was possibly comparatively slow in earlier societies, as the rate of change in present-day, nonliterate societies may be, when compared to the rate characterizing Occidental societies. In any event, rapid changes in behavior are demanded of the person at all levels of social organization even when the society is at its most stable. Life at any level of social development in human societies is a pretty complex business, and it is met and handled most efficiently by those who exhibit the greatest capacity for adaptability, plasticity.

It is this very plasticity of his mental traits which confers upon man the unique position which he occupies in the animal kingdom. Its acquisition freed him from the constraint of a limited range of biologically predetermined responses. He became capable of acting in a more or less regulative manner upon his physical environment instead of being largely regulated by it.

"The immigrant tide must at all costs be stopped and America given a chance to stabilize her ethnic being."

Selective Immigration Is Essential

Lothrop Stoddard

Lothrop Stoddard (1883-1950) was an American writer and lecturer. He had an extensive Harvard education and was admitted to the Massachusetts bar in 1908. A prolific writer on the subject of racism, he stood opposed to a policy permitting unlimited immigration into the United States. In the following viewpoint, Mr. Stoddard explains why he believes that America is doomed unless something is done quickly to place strict limits upon the number of undesirable immigrants allowed into the country.

As you read, consider the following questions:

1. Why does the author call the "melting pot" a fallacy?
2. According to the author, what will happen to America if "racially inferior" immigrants are allowed to continue immigrating into the United States?
3. Why does the author believe that "colored" immigrants pose an even greater danger to America than undesirable European immigrants?

Lothrop Stoddard, *The Rising Tide of Color*. New York: Charles Scribner's Sons, 1920.

[The United States], originally settled almost exclusively by Nordics, was toward the close of the nineteenth century invaded by hordes of immigrant Alpines and Mediterraneans, not to mention Asiatic elements like Levantines and Jews. As a result, the Nordic native American has been crowded out with amazing rapidity by these swarming, prolific aliens, and after two short generations he has in many of our urban areas become almost extinct.

The racial displacements induced by a changed economic or social environment are, indeed, almost incalculable. Contrary to the popular belief, nothing is more *unstable* than the ethnic make-up of a people. Above all, there is no more absurd fallacy than the shibboleth of the "melting-pot." As a matter of fact, the melting-pot may mix but does not melt. Each race-type, formed ages ago, and "set" by millenniums of isolation and inbreeding, is a stubbornly persistent entity. Each type possesses a special set of characters: not merely the physical characters visible to the naked eye, but moral, intellectual, and spiritual characters as well. All these characters are transmitted substantially unchanged from generation to generation....

A Genetic Danger

Now, since the various human stocks differ widely in genetic worth, nothing should be more carefully studied than the relative values of the different strains in a population, and nothing should be more rigidly scrutinized than new strains seeking to add themselves to a population, because such new strains may hold simply incalculable potentialities for good or for evil. The potential reproductive powers of any stock are almost unlimited. Therefore the introduction of even a small group of prolific and adaptable but racially undesirable aliens may result in their subsequent prodigious multiplication, thereby either replacing better native stocks or degrading these by the injection of inferior blood....

The perturbing influence of recent immigration must vex American life for many decades. Even if laws are passed to-morrow so drastic as to shut out permanently the influx of undesirable elements, it will yet take several generations before the combined action of assimilation and elimination shall have restabilized our population and evolved a new type-norm approaching in fixity that which was on the point of crystallizing three-quarters of a century ago.

The biologist Humphrey thus punctures the "melting-pot" delusion: "Our 'melting-pot,' " he writes, "would not give us in a thousand years what enthusiasts expect of it—a *fusing* of all our various racial elements into a new type which shall be the true American. It *will* give us for many generations a perplexing diversity in ancestry, and since our successors must reach back into their ancestry for characteristics, this diversity will increase the uncertainty of their inheritances. They will inherit no stable blended character, because there is no such thing. They will inherit from a mixture of unlike characteristics contributed by unlike peoples, and in their inheritance they will have certain of these characteristics in full identity, while certain others they will not have at all."

America Will Change

Thus, under even the most favorable circumstances, we are in for generations of racial readjustment—an immense travail, essentially needless, since the final product will probably not measure up to the colonial standard. We will probably never (unless we adopt positive eugenic measures) be the race we might have been if America had been reserved for the descendants of the picked Nordics of colonial times.

But that is no reason for folding our hands in despairing inaction. On the contrary, we should be up and doing, for though some of our race-heritage has been lost, more yet remains. We can still be a very great people—if we will it so. Heaven be praised, the colonial stock was immensely prolific before the alien tide wrought its sterilizing havoc. Even to-day nearly one-half of our population is of the old blood, while many millions of the immigrant stock are sound in quality and assimilable in kind. Only—the immigrant tide must at all costs be stopped and America given a chance to stabilize her ethnic being....

America First

Our duty as Americans, interested in the world-wide progress of education, of religious liberty, of democratic institutions, is not only to preserve our own institutions intact, but also to induce the discontented millions of Europe and of Asia to shoulder their own responsibilities at home, there to work out for themselves what our forefathers worked out here for us and for our children. The transfer of European and Asiatic conditions to this country will in the long run help neither ourselves nor foreign countries and their people.

Robert DeCourcy Ward, *The Alien in Our Midst*, 1930.

One fact should be clearly understood: If America is not true to her own race-soul, she will inevitably lose it, and the brightest star that has appeared since Hellas will fall like a meteor from the human sky, its brilliant radiance fading into the night. "We Americans," says Madison Grant, "must realize that the altruistic ideals which have controlled our social development during the past century and the maudlin sentimentalism that has made America 'an asylum for the oppressed,' are sweeping the nation toward a racial abyss. If the melting-pot is allowed to boil without control and we continue to follow our national motto and deliberately blind ourselves to 'all distinctions of race, creed, or color,' the type of native American of colonial descent will become as extinct as the Athenian of the age of Pericles and the Viking of the days of Rollo.''

And let us not lay any sacrificial unction to our souls. If we cheat our country and the world of the splendid promise of American life, we shall have no one to blame but ourselves, and we shall deserve, not pity, but contempt. As Professor Ross well puts it: ''A people that has no more respect for its ancestors and no more pride of race than this deserves the extinction that surely awaits it.''

The Evil Effects

This extended discussion of the evil effects of even white immigration has, in my opinion, been necessary in order to get a proper perspective for viewing the problem of colored immigration. For it is perfectly obvious that if the influx of inferior kindred stocks is bad, the influx of wholly alien stocks is infinitely worse. When we see the damage wrought in America, for example, by the coming of persons who, after all, belong mostly to branches of the white race and who nearly all possess the basic ideals of white civilization, we can grasp the incalculably greater damage which would be wrought by the coming of persons wholly alien in blood and possessed of idealistic and cultural backgrounds absolutely different from ours. If the white immigrant can gravely disorder the national life, it is not too much to say that the colored immigrant would doom it to certain death.

White Man's Veto

This doom would be all the more certain because of the enormous potential volume of colored immigration. Beside it, the white immigrant tide of the past century would pale into insignificance. Leaving all other parts of the colored world out of the present discussion, three Asiatic countries—China, Japan, and India—together have a population of nearly 800,000,000. That is practically twice the population of Europe—the source of white immigration. And the vast majority of these 800,000,000 Asiatics are potential immigrants into white territories. Their standards of living are so inconceivably low, their congestion is so painful, and their consequent desire for relief so keen that the high-standard, relatively empty white world seems to them a perfect paradise. Only the barrier of the white man's veto has prevented a perfect deluge of colored men into white lands, and even as it is the desperate seekers after fuller life have crept and crawled through every crevice in that barrier, until even these advance-guards to-day constitute serious local problems along the white world's race-frontiers.

*"If American ideals...foster human brotherhood
or love culture and liberty, then they are safe with
our new citizens who are eager for these things."*

The US Should Accept All Immigrants

Percy Stickney Grant

Percy Stickney Grant (1860-1927) was a clergyman with a Harvard education and served as rector of the Church of the Ascension in New York from 1893 to 1924. The author of numerous books including *Socialism and Christianity* and *Fair Play for the Worker*, he was an American who spoke out in support of immigration during a time of increasing restrictions. In the following viewpoint, the author argues for allowing foreigners to immigrate to America. He maintains that they would exert a positive influence upon all phases of American life.

As you read, consider the following questions:

1. With what ethnic groups does the author claim to have had personal experience? What does he write about some of those groups?
2. What does the author mean when he writes that "Fusion is a law of progress"?
3. Do you agree with the author? Why or why not?

Percy Stickney Grant, "American Ideals and Race Mixture," *The North American Review*, CXCV, 1912. Reprinted with permission.

The rapidity with which the democratic ideas are taken on by immigrants under the influences of our institutions is remarkable. I have personally had experiences with French-Canadians, Portuguese, Hebrews, and Italians. These races have certainly taken advantage of their opportunities among us in a fashion to promise well for their final effect upon this country. The French-Canadian has become a sufficiently good American to have given up his earlier program of turning New England into a new France—that is, into a Catholic province or of returning to the Province of Quebec. He is seeing something better than a racial or religious ideal in the freedom of American citizenship; and on one or two occasions, when he had political power in two municipalities, he refrained from exercising it to the detriment of the public-school system. He has added a gracious manner and a new feeling for beauty to New England traits....

The actual physical machinery of civilization—cotton-mills, woolen-mills, iron-mills, etc.—lock up a great deal of human energy, physical and mental, just as one hundred years ago the farms did, from which later sprang most of the members of our dominant industrial class. A better organization of society, by which machinery would do still more and afford a freer play for mental and physical energy and organization, would find a response from classes that are now looked upon as not contributing to our American culture; would unlock the high potentialities in the laboring classes, now unguessed and unexpended.

America's Ideals

The intellectual problems and the advanced thinking of the Hebrew, his fondness for study, and his freedom on the whole from wasteful forms of dissipation, sport, and mental stagnation, constitute him a more fortunate acquisition for this country than are thousands of the descendants of colonial settlers. In short, we must reconstruct our idea of democracy—of American democracy. This done, we must construct a new picture of citizenship. If we do these things we shall welcome the rugged strength of the peasant or the subtle thought of the man of the Ghetto in our reconsidered American ideals. After all, what are these American ideals we boast so much about? Shall we say public schools, the ballot, freedom? The American stock use private schools when they can afford them; they too often leave town on election day; as for freedom, competent observers believe it is disappearing. The conservators and believers in American ideals seem to be our immigrants. To the Russian Jew, Abraham Lincoln is a god. If American ideals are such as pay honor to the intellectual and to the spiritual, or foster human brotherhood or love culture and promote liberty, then they are safe with our new citizens who are eager for these things.

Not only do these races bring with them most desirable qualities, but they themselves are subjected to new environment and

67

Immigrant mother and family disembarking at New York City, March 2, 1921.

United Press International, Inc.

strongly influential conditions. Just here arise duties for the present masters of America. Ought they not to create an industrial,

social and educational environment of the most uplifting sort for our foreign-born citizens?

If working-people are obliged to live in unhealthful tenements situated in slums or marsh land, if the saloon is allowed to be their only social center, if they are fought by the rich in every effort to improve their condition, we may expect any misfortune to happen to them and also any fate to befall the state.

What improved *milieu* can do to improving the physique is easily seen on all sides. The increase in the height and weight of Americans in the last few decades is conspicuous. Even the size of American girls and boys has increased, and this increase in size is commonly attributed to the more comfortable conditions of life, to better food, and especially to the popularity of all forms of athletics, and the extension, as in the last twenty-five or thirty years, of the out-of-door and country life. If these factors have made so marked and visible a change in the physique of the children of native-born Americans, why may not the same conditions also contribute an improvement to the more recent immigrant stock?

A New Americanism

Our question, then, as to the effect of race mixture is not the rather supercilious one: What are we admitting into America that may possibly injure American ideals? but, What are the old American races doing to perpetuate these ideals? And is not our future as a race, largely by our own fault, in the hands of the peasant races of Europe?

Indifference, prejudice, illiteracy, segregation of recent immigrants by parochial schools, by a native colonial press, bad physical and social environment, and the low American ideals of citizenship held by those the immigrant sees or hears most about, obstruct race assimilation; but all these can be changed. Yes, it is the keeping up of difference and class isolation that destroys and deteriorates. Fusion is a law of progress.

Every act of religious or civil tyranny, every economic wrong done to races in all the world, becomes the burden of the nation to which the oppressed flee for relief and opportunity. And the beauty of democracy is that it is a method by which these needs may freely express themselves and bring about what the oppressed have prayed for and have been denied. Let us be careful not to put America into the class of the oppressors. Let us rise to an eminence higher than that occupied by Washington or Lincoln, to a new Americanism which is not afraid of the blending in the western world of races seeking freedom. Our present problem is the greatest in our history. Not colonial independence, not federal unity, but racial amalgamation is the heroic problem of the present, with all it implies in purification and revision of old social, religious, and political ideals, with all it demands in new sympathy outside of blood and race, and in a willingness to forego old-time privileges.

"The Japanese can not assimilate and make good citizens because of their racial characteristics, heredity and religion."

The Japanese Are a Menace to America

V.S. McClatchy

V.S. McClatchy (1857-1938), publisher and half-owner of the *Sacramento Bee*, was a well-known California newspaperman. He held several important positions in the communications field, including secretary and general manager of the Pacific Associated Press (1894-1900) and director of the Associated Press (1910-1923). As the executive secretary of the California Joint Immigration Commission in 1923, McClatchy was one of many prominent Californians who opposed continued Japanese immigration to the United States. In the following viewpoint, he explains his opposition.

As you read, consider the following questions:

1. According to the author, in what three ways does Japanese immigration pose a menace to the United States?
2. What is Mikadoism or Shintoism? How does it prevent Japanese from becoming American citizens?

V.S. McClatchy, "Japanese in the Melting-Pot: Can They Assimilate and Make Good Citizens?" *The Annals of the American Academy of Political and Social Science*, January 1921.

There are three principal elements in the menace threatened by Japanese immigration to this country. They are:

1. The non-assimilability of the Japanese race; the practical impossibility of making out of such material valuable and loyal American citizens.

2. Their unusually large birth-rate per thousand population, already shown in California to be three times that of the whites, notwithstanding that the estimated proportion of adult females to males among the Japanese is only 1 to 4, while among the whites it is, say, 1 to 1.

3. The great advantages which they possess in economic competition, partly due to racial characteristics, and partly to standards of living, organization, direction and aid from their government. These advantages make it hopeless for American whites to compete with them.

It should be evident that we can not encourage or permit in our midst the development of an alien element possessing these characteristics without inviting certain disaster to our institutions and to the nation itself. The evidence on each of these points is apparently incontrovertible.

As to non-assimilability, the first element mentioned in the Japanese menace, there are three main reasons why it is useless to attempt the making of good American citizens out of Japanese material, save of course in exceptional individual instances....

1. The Japanese *can not* assimilate and make good citizens because of their racial characteristics, heredity and religion.

2. The Japanese *may not* assimilate and make good citizens because their Government claims all Japanese, no matter where born, as its citizens.

3. The Japanese *will not* assimilate and make good citizens. In the mass, with opportunity offered, and even when born here, they have shown no disposition to do so, but, on the contrary, pronounced antagonism....

Different Religious Ideals

The Japanese hold that their Mikado is the one living God to whom they owe their very existence, and therefore all obedience. It is not possible to make of an individual in whom that belief is deeply and firmly grounded an American citizen who can be relied upon in a crisis. This worship of the Mikado (Mikadoism, or Shinto-ism) is a part of the education of each child in Japan, and school children are by government decree forced to worship at the Shinto shrines....

From a writer long resident in Japan, and fully conversant with its language, its religion and its people, is quoted the following statement on this matter: "Mikadoism, or Emperor worship, is the sheet anchor of patriotic fervor in Japan—the soul of the body politic. The vast majority of the people have no other religion. It is not a relic

71

of bygone days, but the very heart of present-day Japan."

The plea of Sidney Gulick and a number of his Christian friends that we make citizens of the Japanese and then trust to making good citizens of them by Christianizing them, advocates an experiment dangerous in the extreme, doubtful even as to a superficial change in religion, and certain to end in disaster.

Preserving Pure Blood

I believe that one such man as Washington, or Newton, or Franklin, or Lincoln glorifies the Creator of the world and benefits mankind more than all the Chinese who have lived, and struggled, and died on the banks of the Hoang Ho. But it is said that in order to extend the benefits of republican government and free institutions to other peoples, we must admit to citizenship in this land men of all races and classes without distinction. I believe that the surest way to popularize and extend the blessings of civil liberty, free government, and American institutions is by example. Let us keep pure the blood which circulates through our political system; dignify, ennoble, and exalt our sovereign —the people; preserve our national life from the gangrene of oriental civilization.

Senator John Franklin Miller of California, *Congressional Record*, February 28, 1882.

The inherent incapacity of the Japanese for assimilation, their religious belief and ideals, bred in them for generations and taught to them the world over, which foreign birth and foreign residence do not modify, create a permanent and insurmountable barrier between them and that real American citizenship which would be of value, and not a grave menace, to this nation. They can not be transmuted into good American citizens.

Their Allegiance Is Abroad

The second point made by me against the possibility of making American citizens out of Japanese is based upon my statement that Japan does not permit it. We come now to the curious and inconsistent policy of our Government as to dual citizenship, the full viciousness of which is most apparent in the case of the Japanese. We recognize as an American citizen and extend all rights and privileges as such to any one born under the American flag, including, of course, the Japanese. Japan, on the other hand, rigidly insists that every Japanese, no matter where his parents were born, and no matter what nation may have conferred citizenship on him, with or without his request, is a Japanese citizen, and must perform all the obligations as such.

Every Japanese born here, even if his forbears for generations were born here, but had not been permitted to expatriate, is subject to orders from Japan; is kept track of through the Japanese Con-

72

sulate and other organizations, and is subject to call for military duty....

We are thus conferring upon the Japanese born here all the rights and privileges of citizenship, without any of the obligations; and we are certainly breeding in our midst a class of American citizens whose hand, we know in advance, must be against us in possible case of war....

The Japanese children born under the American flag are compelled to attend Japanese schools, usually after the public school hours, where they are taught the language, the ideals and the religion of Japan, with its basis of Mikado worship. Here they are taught by Japanese teachers, usually Buddhist priests, who frequently speak no English, and who almost invariably know nothing of American citizenship. The text-books used are the Mombusho series, issued under the authority of the Department of Education at Tokyo. These schools are located wherever there are Japanese communities, and teachers in the American public schools testify that the Japanese children frequently are studying their Japanese lessons in their public school hours....

Not Disposed to Become Real Americans

It has been shown already why the Japanese *can not* make good citizens, because of their religion and heredity and non-assimilability; it has been shown also why they *may not* make good citizens, because the laws of Japan, efficiently and rigorously administered in the United States, as well as in Japan, do not permit them; it is equally true that they *will not* make good citizens, and that the evidence of the acts of those who have resided under the American Flag for many years is conclusive on this point.

In Hawaii, where their numbers make them independent, and where they are now in a position to practically control the Territory, the Japanese form a separate, alien community, observing the laws, customs and the ideals of Japan; using the Japanese language, both in their business and in their schools, and bringing up their children to be not American but Japanese citizens, with all that loyalty to the Mikado which is a part of the Japanese religion.

The statement made as to Japanese policy in Hawaii is equally true of the Japanese in California, though, because of differences in conditions, the evidence has not forced itself as yet so strongly on public attention. The Japanese schools are found in every Japanese community in California where there are enough children to support them.

The Japanese, however, are not content to depend upon education of their American-born children in this country in order to make them loyal subjects of the Mikado. In the report of the Japanese Association of America, concerning its California census as quoted by the State Board of Control, appears the statement that there are in Japan at this time about 5,000 California-born Japanese.

73

That statement carries little significance to most people. It means, however, that there are at this time 5,000 of the Japanese born in California, that is to say, 20 per cent of California's Japanese minors, upon whom the United States conferred citizenship, who are now back in Japan being thoroughly instructed in the religion and ideals of Japan; so that when they return here they may serve, not as American citizens, but as loyal subjects of the Mikado, to do his will and serve his interests....

The Differences Prevent Assimilation

One reason why the Japanese show no disposition to American-ize themselves lies in their belief, passed down through generations, grounded into them in their schools, and a part of their religion (For is not their nation the only one on earth whose ruler is the living God?), that they are superior to any race on earth. Why, then, should they be willing to expatriate themselves and become citizens of an inferior nation?

The cockiness which many have noticed in the Japanese under certain conditions and on certain occasions, their pride and sensitiveness, their intolerance of criticism or opposition, are all due to this inbred and firmly established belief in their superiority. In the issue on June 10, 1920, of *The Northman*, a Swedish publication printed at Portland, Oregon, Miss Frances Hewett, who spent six years in Japan teaching English to Japanese school children in the public schools there, says: "Neither do the tourists learn that these children are taught that they, being children of the Son of Heaven, are superior to all foreigners, and that their natural destiny is to bring all other peoples to subjection."

Under such conditions, it is not only probable but practically certain that the majority of Japanese who are now endeavoring to secure for themselves the privileges of American citizenship, are doing it not from any desire to help the American nation, or to become an integral part of it, but that they may better serve Japan and the Mikado.

"The Japanese in America...are most sincerely endeavoring to so order their lives as to conform to the economic, social and spiritual ideas and institutions of America."

The Japanese Are Not a Menace to America

Kiichi Kansaki

In the face of growing opposition to the Japanese presence in the United States (especially California), the Japanese Association of America was formed to both defend and enhance the image of the Japanese immigrant in America. A general secretary of the Association, Kiichi Kansaki was one of the Japanese-Americans' most forceful and articulate spokesmen. In 1921, he authored *California and the Japanese*, in which he offered compelling arguments for the acceptance of Japanese-Americans into the political, economic, and social life of the nation. In the following viewpoint, the author attempts to explain the irrationality of anti-Japanese sentiment in America.

As you read, consider the following questions:

1. Why does the author say that anti-Japanese attitudes are irrational?
2. How does he support his contention that physical and cultural assimilation will be no problem for the Japanese?
3. How does he define the Japanese Association of America?

Kiichi Kansaki, "Is the Japanese Menace in America a Reality?" *The Annals of the American Academy of Political and Social Science*, January 1921.

In recent years, and particularly during the past twelve months, a very great deal has been said concerning a Japanese menace in America. Does such a menace in fact exist?...

Recognition of the Japanese problem socially and politically began in America about the year 1900. The typical attitude of that day finds expression in the retiring message of Governor Gage of California, which gave warning of an incoming of Japanese immigrants who were similar in the quality of inferiority with the Chinese, and who maintained the same low standards of wages and living. But that attitude soon changed, and with Japan's successful emergence from the war, with Russia, America commenced to recognize the different and superior qualities of the Japanese as compared to the Chinese. President Roosevelt, in a message to Congress, made special mention of this matter, and although he by no means favored a rapid mingling of the American and Japanese races, he remarked the advantages that might accrue from mutual contact and friendly relations.

Thus, the attitude toward the Japanese has changed with the passing of time, and since the new outburst of anti-Japanese agitation, and particularly since early in 1919, a new position has been taken, namely, that the Japanese are unassimilable, and hence, undesirable, despite their generally admitted good qualities. Thus we find a lack of rationality in anti-Japanese criticism because of the radically different and contradictory arguments that have been advanced. This changing and contradictory tendency to a considerable extent reflects the superficialness and weakness of the argument and attitude of the anti-Japanese agitators who, in their capricity and to influence the indifferent and uninformed public, have used different arguments at different times and for different occasions....

High Birth Rate Not a Racial Trait

For the purpose of discovering what the actual degree of the so-called menace may be I will treat of the population, birth-rate and economic activities of the Japanese in this country; and as two-thirds of all the Japanese in continental America live in California, I will use California facts and statistics as typical of the whole situation....

The high birth-rate among the Japanese in California has furnished one of the main arguments of the anti-Japanese agitators. Mr. V.S. McClatchy, for example, has by foolishly conceived figures sought to show that a continuance of the present birth-rate will mean that in the near future the Japanese in California will outnumber the whites. Such arguments, being almost wholly imaginative, have no practical relation with actuality, and are designed only to appeal to the more ignorant masses by arousing fear and excitement. Necessarily, they are valueless to the scientific investigator. Even the report of the State Board of Control which shows the Japanese birth-rate to be 46.44 and that of the whites to be 16.59, respectively, per thousand population, has furnished no scientific basis for comparison. Such elementary facts as sex distribution, marital conditions, age group and age composition, intellectual status and social environment, have not been supplied; nor has there been made any comparison between the birth-rate of the Japanese and that of other immigrant races, or that obtaining among the whites of the same age group, intellectual status and financial condition. It is obvious that before any authoritative comparison can be made the foregoing data should be assembled and carefully examined....

But granting for the sake of argument that in the past the Japanese birth-rate has been high, there is still nothing unnatural or abnormal about it, for history of all immigration shows that the birth-rate and death-rate of every new immigrant group have at first been high, but that as prosperity and higher standards of living have come to prevail, as the immigrant group has adapted itself to the new environment and different conditions of life, the birth-rate has steadily declined. Also, nearly all immigrants come from large families and hence their first generation is biologically prolific....

Moreover, a high birth-rate is not a racial trait of the Japanese, and as those in this country emerge from their present status, as they are doing very rapidly, their birth-rate will undoubtedly recede to the normal. At any rate, we can not with reason or pro-

Japanese-Americans taken into custody at San Pedro, California, after the bombing of Pearl Harbor, December 7, 1941.
Wide World Photos

priety judge the future by the past; and with the productivity of the Japanese women decreasing with their increasing age, and with new arrivals practically stopped through the cessation of picture-bride immigration, it is not too much to say that in the very near future there will be a marked decline in the Japanese birth-rate.

The agricultural activities of the Japanese have been widely commented upon and made the basis of an effort to prove that farm land in California is rapidly passing into Japanese ownership or control. The actual facts in this regard are particularly illuminating, serving as they do to refute another of the favorite accusations of the anti-Japanese agitators. The total land area of California amounts to 98,000,000 acres, of which 28,000,000 is farm land. Of this, the Japanese own or are buying on contract, individually and through American-Japanese corporations, 74,769 acres, and lease, or operate under crop contracts, 383,287 acres. Thus it appears that the total farm land *occupied* by the Japanese is no more than 1.6 per cent of the total, and that the amount *owned* by them and, hence, *controlled*, is less than one-third of one per cent of the vast farm land area of the state, relatively nothing more than a mere handful. As to the character of the farm land owned by the Japanese, without going into detail, suffice it to say that it is rich and productive—as has been charged—but that it has been made so by the incessant toil of the Japanese who, in most instances, took land either abandoned or regarded as practically useless by others, and made it highly productive.

Physical Assimilation

In bringing this discussion to a consideration of the social and inner qualities of the Japanese in America, we come to the most important phase of the Japanese problem, namely, the question of assimilation....

Assimilation may be defined, for practical purposes and without much emphasis upon its dogmatic phases, as that art or process by which one is brought into a resemblance, harmony, conformity or identity with regard to others. More specifically to our case, it means adjustment to the new conditions and adaptation to the social, political, industrial and cultural institutions, both traditional and actual, of America....

The whole question of assimilation naturally divides into two phases, namely, physical and cultural. The physical assimilation of any race is difficult to measure or to definitely determine, but the fallacy of such an assertion as that "the Creator made the two races different, and different they will remain," has been convincingly demonstrated even by the Immigration Commission. It is not fully recognized that the social, economic and political conditions of America have gradually changed the habits, living customs and modes of thought of the European immigrants who

thus become Americans. Even physical changes affecting heig
weight, the cephalic index, color of hair, etc., have been definit
established. These changes now are taking place also among
Japanese immigrants. Their hair, formerly jet black, is ton
toward the brown and their skin is losing its darker pigment, w
in stature and weight there has been a marked proportion gain;
although there has been no such careful study as would perm
announcing a final conclusion, certainly it can be positively st
that such racial differences as exist between the Japanese an
whites, even if they do tend to discourage a rapid amalgan
by no means prevent even physical assimilation, and tha
connection to the Japanese immigrants are in no different
from all other immigrants....

Cultural Assimilation

As to the cultural assimilation of the Japanese in Am
results are more thoroughly apparent. For instance,
American-born Japanese children. They speak English a
tirely, and in their customs, spirit and mode of thought ar
American than Japanese. They have little desire even to
for America is indeed "home" to them, and their love
and adherence to its ideals is established by the ea
which they have joined and are joining the Boy Scou
and kindred organizations.

Immigrants Are Amer

Oscar Handlin has said, "Once I though
migrants in America. Then I discover
American history." In the same sense, w
ticular "immigrant contribution" to A
have been immigrants or the descend
dians...migrated to the American c
people whose roots in America are ol
immigration left its own imprint on Am
distinctive "contribution" to the building
tion of American life. Indeed, if, as some of the old
to do, we were to restrict the definition of immigrants
people who came to the United States after the De
dependence, we would have to conclude that our h
society would have been vastly different if they all had sta

John F. Kennedy, *A Nation of Immigrants*, 1963.

During the Great War the American-born Japanese
of the requisite age admirably demonstrated that thr
runs a devout love for the stars and stripes and Ameri
encouraging results are found also among the adul

dents, who, by their ideas—social, economic, political and
ural—have demonstrated their complete conversion to the
rican ideal. No better proof of this can be found than the almost
rying tendency of those who go to Japan to soon become
tisfied there and return to America, and of the firm determina-
f almost all of the parents to educate their children in America
ericans, useful for America's future. Again, their mode of
, their ideas, in fact their entire philosophy are being
canized so profoundly that they find no difficulty in per-
their new civic duties and conforming to the American
em. Their devotion to America is further evidenced by the
ess, yes the eagerness, with which they bought their full
liberty bonds, war savings stamps, etc., and made their
contributions to the Red Cross and other war charities.
ese are also rapidly conforming to the spiritual ideals of
r, except in rare instances, the observance of Sunday is
ir life, and their homes and home customs are rapidly
...

Wages, Schools, and Religious Training

anese are willing to work longer hours and accept
than the whites is by no means a true statement.
ed in twenty-two counties show that while in some
cept a lower wage, in others they demand
general average of the hour and wage
between the Japanese and the whites
work. In this regard there is often a
Japanese farm hands, and Japanese
who, like many American farmers,
esire....
ls have occasioned a great deal of
much adverse criticism: misunder-
public has not known their pur-
use the agitators have claimed that
japanese ideas and customs, and
. The real purpose of these schools,
the Japanese language to children who show
nce for and adaptability toward English, in order
ng tie between the parents (who naturally have
king and understanding English) and the children
estroyed. Sever this tie, and the parent must suffer,
ly through the child that he becomes acquainted with
e to the customs and institutions of American life. It
asic idea that the Japanese language schools exist. The
y of them employ American teachers for the smaller
that they are revising their text-books to conform to
rinciples furnishes proof that their teaching and
not other than loyal to America, and evidences the fact

ht,
ely
the
hing
hile
and
it of
ated
d the
nation,
t in this
position

erica the
take the
lmost en-
e far more
visit Japan,
or America
gerness with
ts of America

ican History

t to write a history of the im-
ed that the immigrants were
ve cannot really speak of a par-
merica because all Americans
ants of immigrants; even the In-
ontinent. We can only speak of
der or newer. Yet each wave of
erican society; each made its
of the nation and the evolu-
der immigrants like
o the 42 million
claration of In-
istory and our
ved at home.

young men
ough them
ca. Highly
Japanese

resi
cult
Ame
unva
dissa
tion o
as An
living
Ameri
forming
legal syst
willingn
quota of
generous
The Japan
America fo
part of the
improving.

That the Ja
lower wages
Figures gathere
instances the Japanese
a higher one, and that
scale is practically the
performing the same k
failure to distinguish b
who own their own far
work as long hours as

The Japanese langua
misunderstanding and
standing has arisen be
pose; and adverse critic
such institutions teac
loyalty to the Empire o
however, is to teach
a marked prefere
that the connecti
difficulty in spea
may not be c
for it is maini
and agreeab
is upon this b
fact that mar
children and
American p
precepts are

that these schools, far from being a bar, are of genuine aid to the process of Americanization. The average attitude of the Japanese parent is to so bring up his children so that they will make the best of American citizens, participating in American life and contributing their distinct share to this cosmopolitan civilization.

The religious training of the Japanese is not being neglected, and in this there is a well-recognized tendency toward the Christian religion, Buddhism being rapidly on the wane among the second generation, particularly. There are only twenty-five Buddhist Temples in all of continental America, while on the Pacific Coast, exclusive of Canada, there are sixty-one Protestant Japanese churches, besides a number of Catholic churches, and all of them are gaining in membership and strength. Also, few of the Japanese born here accept other than the Christian faith.

The Japanese Will Become Americanized

An organization that is devoted to raising all of the standards of the Japanese in this country and of genuinely aiding Americanization is the Japanese Association of America with headquarters at San Francisco, which has been in existence since 1900. It has a membership of 16,000 Japanese, all of whom recognize and approve the principles and purposes of the organization. It has taken the lead in all movements designed to promote a better understanding between the Americans and the Japanese here, and to inculcate in the hearts and minds of the latter a devotion to and an understanding of the spirit of America....

In spite of the criticisms of the anti-Japanese agitators, and the prejudices thereby aroused, the Japanese in America, heeding the teachings of their leaders, are most sincerely endeavoring to so order their lives as to conform to the economic, social and spiritual ideas and institutions of America. Therefore, the real and fundamental problem is how to make the Japanese already here an integral part of American society. In this regard, the attitude and program of the anti-Japanese agitators would furnish nothing that would work to the ultimate good of the commonwealth. Instead of such agitation, America should meet the problem with an attitude predicated on the policy of how to Americanize and assimilate the Japanese that are here, so that they may not be left as a foreign and isolated group in America. This, of course, means granting to those who are qualified the rights and privileges of American citizenship.

"Both the intelligence and the prosperity of our working people are endangered by the present immigration."

Immigrant Literacy Tests Are Necessary

Samuel Gompers

Samuel Gompers (1850-1924) was one of the most influential labor leaders in American history. One of the principal architects and the first president of the American Federation of Labor, he devoted his life to upgrading the wages, working conditions and general freedoms of the American worker. However, as an enormous number of immigrants began entering the United States from Europe at the beginning of the twentieth century, Gompers and others viewed this massive influx of new workers as a threat to organized labor. Fearing that the wages and working conditions of union workers would suffer from the increased labor force, Gompers began lobbying for mandatory literacy tests for immigrants. The following viewpoint is taken from a letter Gompers sent to James E. Watson, a congressman from Georgia who supported literacy tests for immigrants.

As you read, consider the following questions:

1. Why does the author favor literacy tests for immigrants?
2. Do you agree with the author? Why or why not?

Samuel Gompers, from a letter of May 16, 1902, quoted in the *Publications of the Immigration Restriction League*, no. 35.

I have observed with much pleasure your activity in the cause of the regulation of immigration, and in particular your introduction of a bill providing that no adult immigrant shall be admitted to our country till he has acquired the first rudiments of education. It is for this reason that I now address you with regard to pending and prospective legislation.

The organized workers of the country feel that the existing immigrations laws, while not without their value, are of trifling effect compared with the needs and the just demands of American labor....

Intelligence and Prosperity

The strength of this country is in the intelligence and prosperity of our working people. But both the intelligence and the prosperity of our working people are endangered by the present immigration. Cheap labor, ignorant labor, takes our jobs and cuts our wages.

The fittest survive; that is, those that fit the conditions best. But it is the economically weak, not the economically strong, that fit the conditions of the labor market. They fit best because they can be got to work cheapest. Women and children drive out men, unless either law or labor organization stops it. In just the same way the Chinaman and others drive out the American, the German, the Irishman.

The tariff keeps out cheap foreign goods. It is employers, not workingmen, that have goods to sell. Workingmen sell labor, and cheap labor is not kept out by the tariff. The protection that would directly help the workers is protection against the cheap labor itself.

Protect Our Own

The Nashville convention of the American Federation of Labor, by a vote of 1,858 to 352, pronounced in favor of an educational test for immigrants. Such a measure would check immigration in a moderate degree, and those who would be kept out by it are those whose competition in the labor market is most injurious to American workers. No other measure which would have any important effect of this kind is seriously proposed.

The need of regulation may be less sharply felt at the present time, when there are less men out of work than there were a few years ago. But the flood of cheap labor is increasing, and its effect at the slightest stagnation in industry or in any crisis will be fearful to the American workmen.

Hard Times

A fall in wages or a relative fall of wages makes the workers unable to buy as large a share as before of the goods they produce. This hastens the time when overproduction or underconsumption will show itself. That means hard times; and when hard times come, the mass of immigrants that prosperity attracted will be here to increase the burden of unemployment.

For these reasons the American Federation of Labor believes that the present opportunity ought not to be allowed to pass without the adoption of an effective measure for the protection of American labor.

A Serious Proposal

The Nashville convention of the American Federation of Labor, by a vote of 1,858 to 352, pronounced in favor of an educational test for immigrants. Such a measure would check immigration in a moderate degree, and those who would be kept out by it are those whose competition in the labor market is most injurious to American workers.

Samuel Gompers.

I earnestly hope that you will be able to procure the embodiment of an illiteracy test for immigrants in the bill (H.R. 12199) which the House now has under consideration.

"Those who come seeking opportunity are not to be admitted unless they have already had one of the chief opportunities they seek, the opportunity of education."

Immigrant Literacy Tests Are Wrong

Woodrow Wilson

Woodrow Wilson (1856-1924) was the 28th President of the United States. As the first non-clerical head of Princeton University, he strove to raise academic standards by providing for more individualized instruction. In 1919, he received the Nobel Prize for peace. His efforts to create a new world society, which would be governed by the "self-determination of peoples," provided the basis for the establishment of the League of Nations. Despite his controversial policies, he is recognized as one of the pivotal figures of American and world history. In the following viewpoint, President Wilson offers several reasons why he believes that the immigrant literacy test bill before Congress should not be passed.

As you read, consider the following questions:

1. In what two ways does the president believe that the literacy test bill departs from traditional US policy?
2. Do you agree with the author? Why or why not?

Woodrow Wilson, from a message to Congress accompanying his veto of January 28, 1915.

In two particulars of vital consequence this bill embodies a radical departure from the traditional and long-established policy of this country, a policy in which our people have conceived the very character of their Government to be expressed, the very mission and spirit of the nation in respect of its relations to the peoples of the world outside their borders. It seeks to all but close entirely the gates of asylum which have always been open to those who could find nowhere else the right and opportunity of constitutional agitation for what they conceived to be the natural and inalienable rights of men; and it excludes those to whom the opportunities of elementary education have been denied, without regard to their character, their purposes, or their natural capacity.

Noble Character

Restrictions like these, adopted earlier in our history as a Nation, would very materially have altered the course and cooled the humane ardors of our politics. The right of political asylum has brought to this country many a man of noble character and elevated purpose who was marked as an outlaw in his own less fortunate land, and who has yet become an ornament to our citizenship and to our public councils. The children and the compatriots of these illustrious Americans must stand amazed to see the representatives of their Nation now resolved, in the fullness of our national strength and at the maturity of our great institutions, to risk turning such men back from our shores without test of quality or purpose. It is difficult for me to believe that the full effect of this feature of the bill was realized when it was framed and adopted, and it is impossible for me to assent to it in the form of which it is here cast.

Unfair Bias

The literacy test and the tests and restrictions which accompany it constitute an even more radical change in the policy of the Nation. Hitherto we have generously kept our doors open to all who were not unfitted by reason of disease or incapacity for self-support or such personal records and antecedents as were likely to make them a menace to our peace and order or to the wholesome and essential relationships of life. In this bill it is proposed to turn away from tests of character and of quality and impose tests which exclude and restrict; for the new tests here embodied are not tests of quality or of character or of personal fitness, but tests of opportunity. Those who come seeking opportunity are not to be admitted unless they have already had one of the chief of the opportunities they seek, the opportunity of education. The object of such provisions is restriction, not selection.

If the people of this country have made up their minds to limit the number of immigrants by arbitrary tests and so reverse the policy of all the generations of Americans that have gone before them, it is their right to do so. I am their servant and have no license to stand in their way. But I do not believe that they have. I respectfully submit that no one can quote their mandate to that effect. Has any political party ever avowed a policy of restriction in this fundamental matter, gone to the country on it, and been commissioned to control its legislation? Does this bill rest upon the conscious and

Political Asylum

The right of political asylum has brought to this country many a man of noble character and elevated purpose who was marked as an outlaw in his own less fortunate land, and who has yet become an ornament to our citizenship and to our public councils. The children and the compatriots of these illustrious Americans must stand amazed to see the representatives of their Nation now resolved, in the fullness of our national strength and at the maturity of our great institutions, to risk turning such men back from our shores without test of quality or purpose.

Woodrow Wilson.

universal assent and desire of the American people? I doubt it. It is because I doubt it that I make bold to dissent from it. I am willing to abide by the verdict, but not until it has been rendered. Let the platforms of parties speak out upon this policy and the people pronounce their wish. The matter is too fundamental to be settled otherwise.

Recognizing Ethnocentrism

Ethnocentrism is the attitude or tendency of people to view their own race, religion, culture, group, or nation as superior to others, and to judge others on that basis. An American, whose custom is to eat with a fork or spoon, would be making an ethnocentric statement when saying, "The Chinese custom of eating with chopsticks is stupid."

Ethnocentrism has promoted much misunderstanding and conflict. It emphasizes cultural and religious differences and the notion that one's national institutions or group customs are superior.

Ethnocentrism limits people's ability to be objective and to learn from others. Education in the truest sense stresses the similarities of the human condition throughout the world and the basic equality and dignity of all people.

Some of the following statements are taken from the viewpoints in this book. Others have other sources. Consider each statement carefully. *Mark E for any statement you think is ethnocentric. Mark N for any statement you think is not ethnocentric. Mark U if you are undecided about any statement.*

If you are doing this activity as a member of a class or group, compare your answers with those of other class or group members. Be able to defend your answers. You may discover that others will come to different conclusions than you. Listening to the reasons others present for their answers may give you valuable insights in recognizing ethnocentric statements.

If you are reading this book alone, ask others if they agree with your answers. You too will find this interaction very valuable.

> *E = ethnocentric*
> *N = not ethnocentric*
> *U = undecided*

1. The new immigration contains a large and increasing number of the weak, the broken, and the mentally crippled of all races drawn from the lowest stratum of the Mediterranean basin and the Balkans.

2. When human beings are brought up in an American environment they become Americans.

3. White children brought up by Chinese exhibit the cultural traits of the environment in which they were culturally conditioned.

4. The man of the old stock is being crowded out of many country districts by these foreigners, just as he is being driven off the streets of New York City by the swarms of Polish Jews.

5. "Ethnic group genes" seem to make no difference in ability to acquire any kind of culture.

6. These immigrants adopt the language of the native [white] American; they steal his name; but they seldom adopt his religion or understand his ideals.

7. The specialized traits of the Nordic man, his splendid fighting and moral qualities, will have little part in the resultant mixture of the melting pot.

8. The American Indian has not acquired the culture of the whites because he has been segregated from that culture on reservations cut off from the main current of American life.

9. Individual success in most human societies depends on ability to fit behavior patterns to societal conditions.

10. All people have a capacity to acquire new behavior patterns and discard old ones in consequence of training.

11. The Nordic native American has been crowded out with amazing rapidity by these swarming, prolific aliens.

12. The outstanding fact about human beings is that they do change and do so more or less rapidly.

13. We will probably never be the race we might have been if America had been reserved for the descendants of the picked Nordics of colonial times.

14. If the white immigrant can gravely disorder the national life, it is not too much to say that the colored immigrant would doom it to certain death.

15. Only the barrier of the white man's veto has prevented a perfect deluge of colored men into white lands.

Bibliography

The following list of books, periodicals, and pamphlets deals with the subject matter of this chapter.

Tom Bethell — "What Immigration Crisis?" *The American Spectator*, August 1984.

A. Boas — "This Nordic Nonsense," *Forum*, 74 (October 1925).

Current Opinion — "Keep America White," 74, (April 1923).

Madison Grant — "America for the Americans," *Forum*, 74 (September 1925).

Veronika Kot — "Will We Still Be an Immigrant Nation?" *In These Times*, April 24/30, 1985.

Chuck Lane — "Why We Should Welcome Immigration: Open the Door," *The New Republic*, April 1, 1985.

Literary Digest — "Are We Still Anglo-Saxons?" September 9, 1922.

Joseph P. Martino — "Two Hands, One Mouth: Can We Afford to Let in More Immigrants?" *Reason*, September 1984.

The Nation — "Ruling Out the Undesirables," April 23, 1924.

David B. Reimers — *Still the Golden Door: The Third World Comes to America*. New York: Columbia University Press, 1985.

Phyllis Schlafly — "Alien Threat," *The New American*, February 3, 1986.

Julian L. Simon — "How Immigrants Affect Americans' Living Standard: A Debate," The Heritage Lectures, No. 39, May 30, 1984. Available from The Heritage Foundation, 214 Massachusetts Avenue NE, Washington, DC 20002.

World's Work — "Immigrants and Vice," 48, (July 1924): 248.

A. Yezurska — "Soap and Water and the Immigrant," *The New Republic*, February 22, 1919.

Is IQ
Testing Racist?

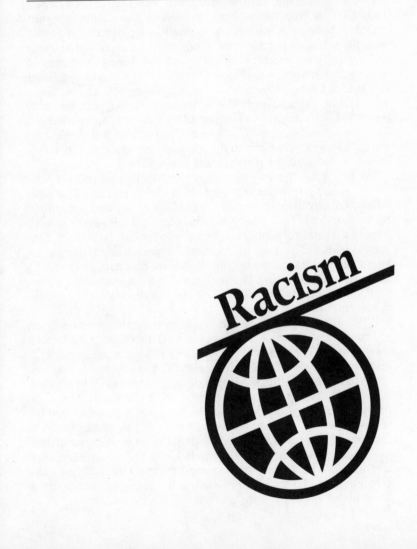

Introduction

At the beginning of the twentieth century, Alfred Binet (1857-1911), a Frenchman, devised a test with which to measure human intelligence. Although originally employed to separate mentally retarded from normal students at an early age, the test eventually was modified to evaluate differing degrees of intelligence in normal children. One difficulty confronting Binet was that of finding a method for standardizing test scores. Since older children almost invariably scored higher than younger ones, a way had to be devised to compensate for the variations resulting from the age differences. This attempt to reconcile test results and age differences gave birth to the intelligence quotient (IQ), a formula for determining intelligence in absolute numbers.

The procedure for formulating a person's IQ is relatively simple. A subject is tested to discover his or her mental age. The mental age is then divided by the chronological age and multiplied by one hundred. Thus, a ten-year-old individual who tests out with a mental age of ten, has an IQ of one hundred. Since one hundred is consider average or "normal," superior or subnormal intelligence is determined by the degree to which an individual's score rises above or falls below the average. (In general, however, an IQ of ten points above or below one hundred is ranked within the normal range.)

While Binet's test gauges the relative performance of a given group on a given test, it cannot reveal the source of human intelligence. The degree to which one's mental aptitude is influenced by inheritance or innate abilities as opposed to environment or learned abilities is impossible to ascertain. Yet for years, IQ test results were interpreted by many as almost infallible indicators of the degree of a person's native intelligence. One of the reasons for this was that test scores were falling in line with the intuitions of the tester. In other words, subjects who were expected to score high performed as anticipated, and vice versa. Moreover, the mass media tended to oversimplify the methodology and interpretation of IQ testing, thereby reinforcing erroneous assumptions about the procedure current among the public.

Since the 1960s, however, the traditional interpretation of IQ has been seriously challenged. The challengers, often referred to as environmentalists, have argued that intelligence is profoundly modified, for better or worse, by life circumstances. Accepting that a certain degree of intelligence is inheritable, the environmentalists maintain that IQ is more indicative of early opportunity and environment than inborn intelligence. Some even conclude that in probably all but the most extreme cases (i.e., the genius and the severely retarded) adequate education can virtually nullify inheritable variations in intelligence.

While the environmentalist position generally has prevailed in academic circles, hereditarianism has experienced a credible resurgence. This revival appears to have originated in an article entitled "How Much Can We Boost I.Q. and Scholastic Achievement?" which appeared in the Winter 1969 issue of the *Harvard Educational Review*. Written by Arthur Jensen, a professor of educational psychology at the University of California (Berkeley), the article stated that IQ and scholastic achievement could not be boosted significantly by compensatory education. Jensen was restating the old hereditarian argument that intelligence is largely inherited. He aggravated the controversy by contending that blacks, as a group, score lower on IQ tests than do whites, and by theorizing that the differences could possibly be attributed to genetic endowment.

Although it had been widely recognized that by and large, blacks do score lower than whites on IQ tests, it was generally agreed that the tests being administered basically reflected white-middle class values and educational background. As such, they were culturally biased and, in the majority of cases, hopelessly unsuited to the black subculture in America. While Jensen advanced studies which he alleged were supportive of his claims, his opponents contended that he simply was parroting outdated and long discredited arguments.

The overwhelming reaction to Jensen was one of strong criticism. He was accused of racism by many of the country's leading social and biological scientists. His classes were picketed and often disrupted by scores of angry students, and several unsuccessful attempts were made to deprive him of his teaching position at Berkeley. (Jensen did have supporters; most notable among them was Richard J. Herrnstein, then chairman of the psychology department at Harvard University.)

The crux of the issue is this: What influence do heredity and environment have upon intelligence? Which of the two factors exerts the greater influence? And, finally, how valid are IQ tests as indicators of intelligence?

While reading the following viewpoints offering both hereditarian and environmentalist views, it might be useful to consider an observation proffered by David Wechsler, a prominent psychologist. The developer of the second most widely used IQ test, Wechsler once noted that the term "intelligence quotient" is, unfortunately, a misnomer. He suggests that it might properly be called "test quotient" (TQ) as, in fact, what it really measures is one's performance on a given test.

"This claim that the black IQ deficit can be blamed on culture-biased...tests does not stand up under rigorous study."

Race and Intelligence Are Related

Arthur Jensen

Arthur Jensen is a professor of educational psychology at the University of California, Berkeley. He received his Ph.D. from Columbia University in 1956. His publications include more than sixty journal articles and several books including *Bias in Mental Testing* and *Straight Talk about Mental Tests*. In the following viewpoint, Dr. Jensen attempts to defend his hypothesis that the genetic differences in intelligence between blacks and whites are real.

As you read, consider the following questions:

1. What does the author believe is the real meaning of racism?
2. What is the genetic hypothesis, according to the author?
3. How does the author describe the performance of blacks on culture-fair and culture-loaded tests?
4. According to the author, what environmental variables don't behave?

Arthur Jensen, "The Differences Are Real," *Psychology Today*, December 1973. Reprinted by permission of *Psychology Today*. Copyright © 1973 Ziff-Davis Publishing Company.

The civil-rights movement that gained momentum in the 1950s "required" liberal academic adherence to the theory that the environment was responsible for any individual or racial behavioral differences, and the corollary belief in genetic equality in intelligence. Thus, when I questioned such beliefs I, and my theories, quickly acquired the label "racist." I resent this label, and consider it unfair and inaccurate.

The Real Meaning of Racism

Since the horrors of Nazi Germany, and Hitler's persecution of the Jews in the name of his bizarre doctrine of Aryan supremacy, the well-deserved offensiveness of the term "racism" has extended far beyond its legitimate meaning. To me, racism means discrimination among persons on the basis of their racial origins in granting or denying social, civil or political rights. Racism means the denial of equal opportunity in education or employment on the basis of color or national origin. Racism encourages the judging of persons not each according to his own qualities and abilities, but according to common stereotypes. This is the real meaning of racism. The scientific theory that there are genetically conditioned mental or behavioral differences between races cannot be called racist. It would be just as illogical to condemn the recognition of physical differences between races as racist.

When I published my article in 1969, many critics confused the purely empirical question of the genetic role in racial differences in mental abilities with the highly charged political-ideological issue of racism. Because of their confusion, they denounced my attempt to study the possible genetic causes of such differences. At the same time, the doctrinaire environmentalists, seeing their own position threatened by my inquiry, righteously and dogmatically scorned the genetic theory of intelligence.

Thankfully, the emotional furor that greeted my article has died down enough recently to permit sober and searching consideration of the true intent and substance of what I actually tried to say. Under fresh scrutiny stimulated by the controversy, many scientists have reexamined the environmentalist explanations of the black IQ deficit and found them to be inadequate. They simply do not fully account for the known facts, in the comprehensive and consistent manner we should expect of a scientific explanation.

The Black IQ Deficit

First of all, it is a known and uncontested fact that blacks in the United States score on average about one standard deviation below whites on most tests of intelligence. On the most commonly used IQ tests, this difference ranges from 10 to 20 points, and averages about 15 points. This means that only about 16 percent of the black population exceeds the test performance of the average white on IQ tests. A similar difference of one standard deviation between blacks and whites holds true for 80 standardized mental tests on which published data exist.

A difference of one standard deviation can hardly be called inconsequential. Intelligence tests have more than proved themselves as valid predictors of scholastic performance and occupational attainment, and they predict equally well for blacks as for whites. Unpleasant as these predictions may seem to some people, their significance cannot be wished away because of a belief in equality. Of course, an individual's success and self-fulfillment depends upon many characteristics *besides* intelligence, but IQ does represent an index, albeit an imperfect one, of the ability to compete in many walks of life. For example, many selective colleges require College Board test scores of 600 (equivalent to an IQ of 115) as a minimum for admission. An average IQ difference of one standard deviation between blacks and whites means that the white population will have about seven times the percentage of such potentially talented persons (i.e., IQs over 115) as the black population. At the other end of the scale, the 15-point difference in average IQ scores means that mental retardation (IQ below 70) will occur about seven times as often among blacks as among whites.

Genes Determine Intelligence

A child's intelligence is influenced more by the genes he inherits than by the environment in which he is reared, a University of Texas study shows. At about midway in a four-year study, three university psychologists—Drs. Joseph Horn, John Loehlin, and Lee Willerman—have found that the IQ levels of adopted children more closely resemble those of their biological mothers [whom the children never knew] than those of the adoptive mothers who have brought them up.

The study, which focuses on the single-born, verifies earlier studies made elsewhere on twins which indicate that heredity is more important to IQ than environment. Dr. Horn is the principal investigator on the Texas Adoption Project, the largest of its kind ever made that uses the IQ levels of biological mothers as its basic reference point.

Intellect, April 1975.

The IQ difference between blacks and whites, then, clearly has considerable social significance. Yet the environmentalists dismiss this difference as artificial and claim it does not imply any innate or genetic difference in intelligence. But as I shall show, the purely environmental explanations most commonly put forth are faulty. Examined closely in terms of the available evidence, they simply do not sustain the burden of explanation that they claim. Of course, they may be *possible* explanations of the IQ difference, but that does not necessarily make them the *most probable*. In every case for which there was sufficient relevant evidence to put to a detailed test, the environmental explanations have proven inadequate. I am not saying they have been proven 100 percent wrong, only that they do not account for *all* of the black IQ deficit. Of course, there may be other possible environmental explanations as yet unformulated and untested.

Arguments for the Genetic Hypothesis

The genetic hypothesis, on the other hand, has not yet been put to any direct tests by the standard techniques of genetic research. It must be seriously considered, however, for two reasons: 1) because the default of the environmentalist theory, which has failed in many of its most important predictions, increases the probability of the genetic theory; 2) since genetically conditioned physical characteristics differ markedly between racial groups, there is a strong *a priori* likelihood that genetically conditioned behavioral or mental characteristics will also differ. Since intelligence and other mental abilities depend upon the physiological structure of the brain, and since the brain, like other organs, is subject to genetic influence, how can anyone disregard the obvious probability of genetic influence on intelligence?

Let us consider some of the genetically conditioned characteristics that we already know to vary between major racial groups: body size and proportions; cranial size and shape; pigmentation of the hair, skin and eyes; hair form and distribution; number of vertebrae; fingerprints; bone density; basic-metabolic rate; sweating; consistence of ear wax; age of eruption of the permanent teeth; blood groups; chronic diseases; frequency of twinning; male-female birth ratio; visual and auditory acuity; color-blindness; taste; length of gestation period; physical maturity at birth. In view of so many genetically conditioned traits that do differ between races, wouldn't it be surprising if genetically conditioned mental traits were a major exception?...

Culture-Fair vs. Culture-Biased

What about the purely cultural and environmental explanations of the IQ difference? The most common argument claims that IQ tests have a built-in cultural bias that discriminates against blacks and other poor minority groups. Those who hold this view criticize the tests as being based unfairly on the language, knowledge and cognitive skills of the white "Anglo" middle class. They argue that blacks in the United States do not share in the same culture as whites, and therefore acquire different meanings to words, different knowledge, and a different set of intellectual skills.

However commonly and fervently held, this claim that the black IQ deficit can be blamed on culture-based or "culture-loaded" tests does not stand up under rigorous study. First of all, the fact that a test is culture-*loaded* does not necessarily mean it is culture-*biased*. Of course, many tests do have questions of information, vocabulary and comprehension that clearly draw on experiences which could only be acquired by persons sharing a fairly common cultural background. Reputable tests, called "culture-fair" tests, do exist, however. They use nonverbal, simple symbolic material common to a great many different cultures. Such tests measure the ability to generalize, to distinguish differences and similarities, to see relationships, and to solve problems. They test reasoning power rather than just specific bits of knowledge.

Genes More Important than Environment

How much of the *variation* among persons in a given population is attributable to the differences in their environments and how much to differences in their genetic endowments?

Numerous studies conducted by psychologists and geneticists over the last 40 or 50 years provide an answer to this question. The answer is unambiguous and is generally agreed upon by all scientists who have considered all the evidence. This evidence strongly supports the conclusion that genetic factors are much more important than environmental influences in accounting for *individual differences* in I.Q. How much more important? The evidence indicates that genetic factors account for at least *twice* as much of the variation in I.Q.'s as environmental factors.

Arthur R. Jensen, *Saturday Evening Post*, Summer 1972.

Surprisingly, blacks tend to perform relatively better on the more culture-loaded or verbal kinds of tests than on the culture-fair type. For example, on the widely used Wechsler Intelligence Scale, comprised of 11 different subtests, blacks do better on the culture-loaded subtests of vocabulary, general information, and verbal comprehension than on the nonverbal performance tests such as the block designs. Just the opposite is true for such minorities as Orientals, Mexican-Americans, Indians, and Puerto Ricans. It can hardly be claimed that culture-fair tests have a built-in bias in favor of white, Anglo, middle-class Americans when Arctic Eskimos taking the same tests perform on a par with white, middle-class norms. My assistants and I have tested large numbers of Chinese children who score well above white norms on such tests, despite being recent immigrants from Hong Kong and having parents who hold low-level socioeconomic occupations. If the tests have a bias toward the white, Anglo, middle-class, one might well wonder why Oriental children should outscore the white Anglos on whom the tests were originally standardized. Our tests of Mexican-Americans produced similar results. They do rather poorly on the culture-loaded types of tests based on verbal skills and knowledge, but they do better on the culture-fair tests. The same holds true for American Indians. All these minorities perform on the two types of tests much as one might expect from the culture-bias hypothesis. Only blacks, among the minorities we have tested, score in just the opposite manner....

Variables That Don't Behave

A host of other environmental variables don't behave as they ought to according to a strictly environmentalist theory of the black IQ deficit. For example, on practically all the socioeconomic, educational, nutritional and other health factors that sociologists point to as causes of the black-white differences in IQ and scholastic achievement, the American Indian population ranks about as far below black standards as blacks do below those of whites. The relevance of these environmental indices can be shown by the fact that within each ethnic group they correlate to some extent in the expected direction with tests of intelligence and scholastic achievement. Since health, parental education, employment, family income, and a number of more subtle environmental factors that have been studied are all deemed important for children's scholastic success, the stark deprivation of the Indian minority, even by black standards, ought to be reflected in a comparison of the intelligence and achievement-test performance of Indians and blacks. But in a nationwide survey reported in the Coleman Report, in 1966, Indians scored *higher* than blacks on all such tests, from the first to the 12th grade. On a nonverbal test given in the first grade, for example, before schooling could have had much impact, Indian children exceeded the mean score of blacks by the equivalent of 14 IQ points. Similar findings occur with Mexican-Americans, who rate below blacks on socioeconomic and other environmental indices, but score considerably higher on IQ tests, especially on the nonverbal type. Thus the IQ difference between Indians and blacks, and between Mexican-Americans and blacks, turns out opposite to what one would predict from purely environmental theory, which of course, assumes complete genetic equality for intelligence. No testable environmental hypothesis has as yet been offered to account for these findings.

Editor's note: On the basis of a study he conducted in a rural Georgia town, Arthur Jensen has modified his position regarding the influence of genetics on IQ. The study showed that the IQ among black students of the community between the ages of five and eighteen underwent a steady decline with age. However, according to Jensen, this "cumulative deficit in IQ...is almost totally due to environmental factors of living in depressed, disadvantaged conditions lower than those of whites in the same area." In the June 18, 1977 issue of Science News, *he is quoted as saying, "This means that the black-white difference, at least in certain parts of the country, does have an environmental cause...."*

"Jensen had no new data; and what he did present was flawed beyond repair."

Race and Intelligence Are Not Related

Stephen Jay Gould

Stephen Jay Gould is a paleontologist who has taught at Harvard University since 1967. The author of numerous books and articles, he is the recipient of several writing awards including the National Book Award in Science (1981) and the National Book Critics Circle Award for General Non-Fiction (1982). In the following viewpoint, the author employs a "hierarchical" chain of logic to refute the arguments of the previous author, Arthur Jensen.

As you read, consider the following questions:

1. According to the author, how does Arthur Jensen rely upon the "natural experiment" of identical twins to support his position?
2. What is the "hierarchical" method used by the author to refute Arthur Jensen's claims?
3. Does the author ultimately reject the idea of intelligence having a genetic basis? Explain your answer.

Stephen Jay Gould, "Racist Arguments and IQ." Reprinted with permission from NATURAL HISTORY, Vol. 83, No. 5; Copyright the American Museum of Natural History, 1974.

Louis Agassiz, the greatest biologist of mid-nineteenth-century America, argued that God had created blacks and whites as separate species. The defenders of slavery took much comfort from this assertion, for biblical proscriptions of charity and equality did not have to extend across a species boundary. What could an abolitionist say? Science had shone its cold and dispassionate light upon the subject; Christian hope and sentimentality could not refute it.

Debate Over the Philippines

During the Spanish-American War, a great debate raged over whether we had the right to annex the Philippines. Imperialists again took comfort from science, for social Darwinism proclaimed a hierarchy in racial ability. When antiimperialists cited Henry Clay's contention that God would not create a race incapable of self-government, Rev. Josiah Strong answered: "Clay's contention was formed before modern science had shown that races develop in the course of centuries as individuals do in years, and that an underdeveloped race, which is incapable of self-government, is no more of a reflection on the Almighty than is an underdeveloped child, who is incapable of self-government."

I cite these examples not merely because they expose science at its most ridiculous, but because they illustrate a far more important point: statements that seem to have the sanction of science have been continually invoked in attempts to equate egalitarianism with sentimental hope and emotional blindness. People who are unaware of this historical pattern tend to accept each recurrence at face value: that is, they assume each such statement arises from the "data" actually presented rather than from the social conditions that truly inspire it.

We have never, I shall argue, had any hard data on genetically based differences in intelligence among human groups. Speculation, however, has never let data stand in its way; and when men in power need such an assertion to justify their actions, there will always be scientists available to supply it.

Craniometry Discredited

The racist arguments of the nineteenth century were primarily based on craniometry, the measurement of human skulls. Today, these contentions stand totally discredited. What craniometry was to the nineteenth century, intelligence testing has been to the twentieth. The victory of the eugenics movement in the Immigration Restriction Act of 1924 signaled its first unfortunate effect—for the severe restrictions upon non-Europeans and upon southern and eastern Europeans gained much support from the results of the first extensive and uniform application of intelligence tests in America—the Army Mental Tests of World War I. These tests were engineered and administered by psychologist Robert M. Yerkes, who concluded that "education alone will not place the negro race

102

[*sic*] on a par with its Caucasian competitors." It is now clear that Yerkes and his colleagues knew no way to separate genetic from environmental components in postulating causes for different performances on the tests.

Attitudes vs. Hard Data

I do not contest the obvious that there are real differences among individuals' psychological traits—such as intelligence—that our society values. But I do suggest that, given the insufficient and controversial quality of the information relevant to the causes of these differences, it is likely that deep personal attitudes rather than logic or sound empirical data dictate one's interpretations of the documented variability in IQ.

Jerome Kagan, *The Saturday Review*, September 4, 1971.

The latest episode of this recurring drama began in 1969, when Arthur Jensen published his article entitled, "How Much Can We Boost I.Q. and Scholastic Achievement?" in the *Harvard Educational Review*. Again, the claim was made that new and uncomfortable information had come to light, and that science had to speak the "truth" even if it refuted some cherished notions of a liberal philosophy. But again, I shall argue, Jensen had no new data; and what he did present was flawed beyond repair by inconsistencies in the data themselves and by illogical claims in his presentation.

Jensen's Assumptions

Jensen assumes that I.Q. tests adequately measure something we may call "intelligence." He attempts to tease apart the genetic and environmental factors causing differences in performance on these tests. He does this by relying upon the one natural experiment we possess: identical twins reared apart—for here the differences can only be environmental. The average difference in I.Q. for such twins is less than the difference for two unrelated individuals raised in similarly varied environments. From the data on twins, he obtains an estimate of the magnitude of environmental influence and estimates the genetic component from the additional differences in I.Q. between unrelated individuals. He concludes that I.Q. has a heritability of about 0.8 (or 80 percent) *within* the population of American and European whites. The average difference between American whites and blacks is 15 I.Q. points (one standard deviation). He asserts that this difference is too big to attribute to environment, given the high heritability of I.Q. Lest anyone think that he writes in the tradition of abstract scholarship, I merely quote the first line of his famous work: "Compensatory education has been tried, and it apparently has failed."

I believe that this argument can be refuted in a "hierarchical" fashion—that is, we can discredit it at one level and then show that it would fail at a more inclusive level even if we allowed Jensen's argument for the first two levels:

Level 1: The equation of I.Q. with intelligence. Who knows what I.Q. measures? It is a good predictor of "success" in school, but is such success a result of intelligence, apple polishing, or the assimilation of values that the leaders of society prefer? Some psychologists get around this argument by defining intelligence as the scores attained on "intelligence" tests. A neat trick. But at this point, the technical definition of intelligence has strayed so far from the vernacular that we no longer can define the issue. But let me allow (although I don't believe it), for the sake of argument, that I.Q. measures some meaningful aspect of intelligence in its vernacular sense.

Different Meanings

Level 2: The heritability of I.Q. Here again, we encounter a confusion between vernacular and technical meanings of the same word. "Inherited," to a layman, means "fixed," "inexorable," or "unchangeable." To a geneticist, "inherited" refers to an estimate of similarity between related individuals based on genes held in common. It carries no implication of inevitability or of immutable entities beyond the reach of environmental influence. Eyeglasses correct a variety of inherited problems in vision; insulin can check diabetes.

Jensen insists that I.Q. is 80 percent heritable. Princeton psychologist Leon J. Kamin has recently done the dog-work of meticulously checking through details of the twin studies that form the basis of this estimate. He has found an astonishing number of inconsistencies and downright inaccuracies. For example, the late Sir Cyril Burt, who generated the largest body of data on identical twins reared apart, pursued his studies of intelligence for more than forty years. Although he increased his sample sizes in a variety of "improved" versions, some of his correlation coefficients remain unchanged to the third decimal place—a statistically impossible situation. Other studies did not standardize properly for age and sex. Since I.Q. varies with these properties, an improper correction may produce higher values between twins not because they hold genes for intelligence in common, but simply because they share the same sex and age. The data are so flawed that no valid estimate for the heritability of I.Q. can be drawn at all. But let me assume (although no data support it), for the sake of argument, that the heritability of I.Q. is as high as 0.8.

Level 3: The confusion of within- and between-group variation. Jensen draws a causal connection between his two major assertions—that the within-group heritability of I.Q. is 0.8 for American whites, and that the mean difference in I.Q. between

American blacks and whites is 15 points. He assumes that the black "deficit" is largely genetic in origin because I.Q. is so highly heritable. This is a *non sequitur* of the worst possible kind—for there is no necessary relationship between heritability within a group and differences in mean values of two separate groups.

IQ Increasing Genes

Jensen has stated that because the gene pools of white and blacks are known to differ and "these genetic differences are manifested in virtually every anatomical, physiological and biochemical comparison one can make between representative samples of identifiable racial groups...there is no reason to suppose that the brain should be exempt from this generalization." But there is no *a priori* reason why genes affecting IQ which differ in the gene pools of whites and blacks, should be such that on the average whites have significantly more genes increasing IQ than blacks do. On the contrary, one should expect, assuming no tendency for high IQ genes to accumulate by selection in one race or the other, that the more polymorphic genes there are that affect IQ and that differ in frequency in blacks and whites, the less likely it is that there is an average genetic difference in IQ between the races. The same argument applies to the differences between any two racial groups.

W.F. Bodmer, *Race, Culture, and Intelligence*, 1972.

A simple example will suffice to illustrate this flaw in Jensen's argument. Height has a much higher heritability within groups than anyone has ever claimed for I.Q. Suppose that height has a mean value of five feet two inches and a heritability of 0.9 (a realistic value) within a group of nutritionally deprived Indian farmers. This high heritability simply means that short farmers will tend to have short offspring, and tall farmers tall offspring. It says nothing whatever against the notion that proper nutrition could raise the mean height to six feet (taller than average white Americans). It only means that, in this improved status, farmers shorter than average (they may now be five feet ten inches) would still tend to have shorter than average children.

No Valid Data

I do not claim that intelligence, however defined, has no genetic basis—I regard it as trivially true, uninteresting, and unimportant that it does. The expression of any trait represents a complex interaction of heredity and environment. Our job is simply to provide the best environmental situation for the realization of valued potential in all individuals. I merely point out that a specific claim purporting to demonstrate a mean genetic deficiency in the intelligence of American blacks rests upon no new facts whatever and can cite no valid data in its support. It is just as likely that blacks have a genetic advantage over whites. And, either way, it doesn't matter a damn. An individual can't be judged by his group mean.

If current biological determinism in the study of human intelligence rests upon no new facts (actually, no facts at all), then why has it arisen from so many quarters of late? The answer must be social and political—and the sooner we realize how much of science is so influenced, the sooner we will demythologize it as an inexorable "truth-making machine." Why now? The 1960s were good years for liberalism; a fair amount of money was spent on poverty programs and relatively little happened. Enter new leaders and new priorities. Why didn't the earlier programs work? Two possibilities are open: (1) we didn't spend enough money, we didn't make sufficiently creative efforts, or (and this makes any established leader jittery) we cannot solve these problems without a fundamental social and economic transformation of society; or (2) the programs failed because their recipients are inherently what they are—blaming the victims. Now, which alternative will be chosen by men in power in an age of retrenchment?

Social and Moral Influences

I have shown, I hope, that biological determinism is not simply an amusing matter for clever cocktail party comments about the human animal. It is a general notion with important philosophical implications and major political consequences. As John Stuart Mill wrote, in a statement that should be the motto of the opposition: "Of all the vulgar modes of escaping from the consideration of the effect of social and moral influences upon the human mind, the most vulgar is that of attributing the diversities of conduct and character to inherent natural differences."

"The problem of differences, in measured intelligence between races, can be a severe one, more severe than many environmentalists are willing to acknowledge."

Genes Help Determine Intelligence

Lloyd G. Humphreys

Lloyd G. Humphreys has had a long and varied academic career since receiving his Ph.D. in psychology from Standford University in 1938. He has held academic positions at Northwestern University, the University of Washington, Stanford University and the University of Illinois, Champaign-Urbana where he has taught since 1957. In 1983, Dr. Humphreys was a member of the expert committee on pediatric neurobehavioral evaluations for the Environmental Protection Agency. In the following viewpoint, he lists and elaborates upon nine generalizations that he believes support his argument that genes and intelligence are interrelated.

As you read, consider the following questions:

1. Why does the author use American blacks and whites as the focus of his study?
2. List the nine generalizations presented by the author.
3. Do you agree with the author? Why or why not?

Lloyd G. Humphreys, "Race and Intelligence Reexamined." This article first appeared in THE HUMANIST issue of July/August 1980 and is reprinted by permission.

My topic is a sensitive and emotionally charged one that both well-meaning and not so well-meaning people on opposite poles of the issue have very strong beliefs about; namely, are observed differences in human intelligence between races largely innate or acquired? Persons taking an extreme position frequently have an axe to grind. Some hereditarians insist on complete separation of the races. At the other extreme, some environmentalists insist on complete and instant equality between races in the areas of education, jobs, and income, in spite of present differences. Both of these extreme groups, as well as many in between, are convinced that solutions to the policy problems lie in the answer to the nature-nurture question. An answer to this question is less important than commonly believed, and the problem of differences, in measured intelligence between races, can be a severe one, more severe than many environmentalists are willing to acknowledge. But steps can be taken to reduce the magnitude of the problem without reaching a decision concerning its causes.

My focus is on American blacks and American whites because of the extensive amount of data available. Neither group constitutes a random sample of blacks and whites worldwide. The data are almost entirely based on a social definition of race that results in placing a larger proportion of white genes in the black gene pool than the reverse. In spite of the admixture, however, there are genetically determined biological differences in physical traits between the socially defined groups. The correlation between the social and biological definitions is still high, though imperfect.

The Genetic Hypothesis

The hypothesis that there is a genetic difference between blacks and whites that is responsible for the measured difference in intelligence requires as a necessary, but not sufficient, condition that there be a genetic contribution to individual differences in intelligence within racially defined groups. I accept the reality of this genetic condition. One must overlook a great deal of evidence, including evolutionary continuity in both behavior and structure, in order to believe that the genetic contribution is zero, although some scientists have been able to do this. They may appropriately be called the Lysenkoists of human genetics. The only reasonable area of doubt concerns the size of the genetic contribution....

The definition of the genetic hypothesis and the concept of intelligence provides us with a framework for the analysis and understanding of some descriptive data concerning American blacks and whites. While these nine generalizations are consistent with the genetic hypothesis, they are also consistent, in one way or another, with environmental hypotheses. While they do not have the same status as the laws of falling bodies in physics, they are similar to the empirical generalizations that come from traditional engineering research. As such, they serve to limit the number

108

and kind of environmental hypotheses that can be used to explain race differences.

1. *How large is the difference?* Setting the mean intelligence quotient of whites at 100, the mean IQ of blacks is about 85. Variability about each mean is quite large, so that about 15 percent of blacks score above the white mean and 15 percent of whites score below the black mean. If we translate IQ into mental age, the average white six-year-old has a mental age of six, while the average black six-year-old has a mental age of five. At age twelve, the respective mental ages are twelve and ten; that is, the mean difference between blacks and whites remains constant with age when measured by IQ, but increases when measured in mental-age units. Nevertheless, the same proportion of blacks are above the white mental-age mean and the same proportion of whites are below the black mental-age mean at all levels. Both blacks and whites are found at all levels of human ability, but in different proportions. These are not trivial differences, but neither do they justify segregation for any social purpose. The size does indicate that possible environmental causes must be potent ones.

Is Ignorance Bliss?

There is, of course, a still more fundamental issue at stake, which should concern even those who are neither curious about nor competent to study racial differences in I.Q. It is whether inquiry shall (again) be shut off because someone thinks society is best left in ignorance.

Setting aside the racial issue, the conclusion about intelligence is that, like other important though not necessarily vital traits, it is highly heritable.

Richard Herrnstein, *The Atlantic Monthly,* September 1971.

---

2. *How broad is the difference?* The difference described above is not restricted to verbal tests of intelligence. Differences as large or larger are found on nonverbal tests of intelligence. As a matter of fact, differences in the same direction, but varying a little in size from one type of test to another, are found on every measure of cognitive function that anyone has used, other than a test of black urban argot. Measures of mechanical information and comprehension that are not well represented in standard tests of intelligence show larger race differences than do verbal tests of intelligence. Use of so-called black English is not a possible explanation for black deficits. The language deficit is equaled, or even exceeded, by many other deficits.

3. *When does the deficit appear?* The black-white difference appears during the preschool period. The size of the difference, in

the only acceptable units of measurement based on the spread of individual differences within the groups, remains approximately constant from the first year in public school to the twelfth year. The schools do not add to, let alone produce, the race difference. On the other hand, they do not correct any part of it.

Note that, at the end of the twelfth year in public schools, the deficit is not merely in scores on intelligence tests. The deficit is of equal magnitude in knowledge of the basics of English composition, in both visual and oral comprehension of English, in basic arithmetic as well as in elementary mathematics, and in knowledge of science, social studies, and the mechanical arts. One-half of black eighteen-year-olds after twelve years of public school have an achievement level in these basic skills below the ninth year of school, or fifteen-year-old level.

4. *Are the schools inferior?* Years ago, Southern schools for blacks were inferior in every way. By the mid-sixties, however, there were no appreciable differences nationwide in the quality of black and white schools, as measured by a variety of objective physical and economic indices. The only appreciable differences were in the racial distributions of students, teachers, and administrators. I am unwilling to blame the failure of the schools to decrease the intellectual deficit on fellow black students, or on black teachers and administrators. Integration of schools can and must be justified on grounds other than the amount of intellectual gain.

Since World War I

5. *Has the deficit decreased?* There has been no apparent decrease in the size of race differences since they were first measured on a wide scale during World War I, even though there has been an increase in the overall American mean during the same time span. An increase in the population mean over time has also been demonstrated in Scotland from the thirties to the late forties. There was a major increase in the number of years of education provided in America in the years following World War I; this is the most probable cause of the increase, but it apparently affected all groups equally.

6. *Are other minority groups equally disadvantaged?* American Orientals score at about the same level as the white majority. In the large-scale survey by James Coleman in 1965, American Indians scored almost as high as Orientals and whites in their first year in public school, but dropped somewhat during the school years. At the end of the twelfth grade, Indian achievement remained higher than black achievement. Yet in terms of several socioeconomic indices—income, housing, and life expectancy—Indians are more disadvantaged than blacks. The white majority at each level of socioeconomic status also scores higher than its black counterpart. These data appear to rule out environmental explanations based on socioeconomic privilege and minority status as such.

110

7. *Do some test questions discriminate against blacks?* Critics have pointed to specific questions on tests as being particularly biased against anyone in the black community. Thus the total score is supposedly depressed by a minority of items of this sort. There is now adequate evidence to contradict such claims. It has been shown that, for a number of different intelligence tests, there is no appreciable bias that varies from item to item. There is more item-to-item bias between white children in London and in San Francisco than between black and white children in San Francisco. What little bias there is in the latter comparison disappears when mental age is controlled.

Two Erroneous Premises

Two basic premises underly the rejection of the concept of genetic inferiority of humans, no matter whether the concept is applied to individuals or to races. One is the American ideal that stems from the "created equal" phrase in the Declaration of Independence. That phrase was intended to apply to social rights but is popularly misinterpreted as equality in genetic endowment. This is biologically ridiculous. It asserts that man alone, of all species of mammals, is made up of individuals all genetically equal—equal at least in potential for socioeconomic success in our society. The second premise is what I have labeled the Apple-of-God's-Eye Obsession. AGEO for short....

AGEO adherents hold that God created all mankind with equal dignity and equal potential, and that God could not have done anything else. These views are so widely held and accepted that they have set up taboos that prevent research. This is an example of berserk humanitarianism.

William Shockley, *Playboy*, August 1980.

The differences between black and white cultures in America have been exaggerated. Children of all races, with the possible exception of some American Indians, go to similar schools, have teachers and administrators with similar training, use the same textbooks, have access to the same newspapers, magazines, radio and television sources, attend the same movies, and so on. Even the differences between black and standard English have been exaggerated. This listing of similarities does not, of course, belie the substantial mean differences in years of education, occupational prestige, and family income between the races. But with 36 percent of black families headed by a lone woman, many of whom are on relief, a substantial amount of the difference between means of the two races in occupational status and family income can be accounted for.

8. *Do white tests predict black performance?* It is widely believed

that tests developed for whites do not predict well for blacks. Such claims have taken two forms: (a) that the correlation (relationship) between test score and future socially important performance is lower for blacks than for whites, and (b) even if the relationship is equally high, blacks will perform on the social criterion at a higher level than their test scores indicate.

The first claim is based on the assumption that cultural differences are so great that the same test cannot be used for both groups. The second assumes that, given the opportunity, native ability will quickly become manifest, and there will be a sudden flowering or burst of achievement. Both beliefs are now known to be false under rather a wide range of conditions. The research consensus is that a test standardized and validated on the white population is equally valid for blacks, as defined by the relationship between test scores and future criterion measures. Furthermore, in a mixed racial group, a given test score somewhat overestimates the future performance of blacks and underestimates the future performance of whites. This is true in education, industry, and the military service, and holds for periods of many months between test administration and later performance. There is no sudden flowering.

The Nature of Intelligence

The expectations, contrary to the results obtained, were based upon a naive view of the nature of intelligence that is probably rather widespread. Intelligence is not like water under pressure where the only problem is to locate and turn the spigot, allowing the liquid to gush forth. Intelligence develops slowly under the influence of both maturation and experience. Not only are abilities acquired during development, but disabilities as well. Tests are culturally loaded, but successful performance in education, occupations, and military assignments is also culturally loaded.

These data that indicate that black performance in education, in the military, and in civilian jobs tend to be overpredicted by the tests on which blacks have lower scores than whites should suffice to refute the claim that black deficits occur only on the tests. Abolishing the use of tests will not abolish the differences.

9. *Are family patterns of intelligence similar?* White parents who have extreme scores in intelligence, in either direction from the mean, have children, on the average, with less extreme scores than themselves; that is, their children regress toward the population mean. The precise amount of regression can be estimated with high accuracy. If one selects only one parent and one child from each family, the correlation between parents and children in intelligence is about .50. Correlations involving both parents and one child are somewhat higher, but the former situation is assumed in making the following quantitative statements. The mean of the children of a group of parents all at 140 IQ will be 120, just halfway back toward the population mean. At the other end of the distribution,

a set of parents all at an IQ of 70 will have children whose mean will be 85. There will be a great deal of variability among the children of these extreme parents around the expected means. Some high-scoring parents will have below-average children, and some low-scoring parents will have above-average children, but the proportions in each case will be small.

Regression to the Mean

Parallel data for blacks are not as firm as for whites, but it appears that the children of extreme black parents regress toward the black mean of 85 by the same proportionate amount. Thus black parents of 140 IQ have children whose mean is 112-113, while black parents of 70 IQ have children whose mean is 77-78. Variability about these expected values is probably similar for the two groups. The implications for an environmental hypothesis are that the effects associated with being black are quite pervasive and extend to the best of black environments.

The phenomena of regression are congruent with the genetic hypothesis, both between and within groups. The amount observed is the amount expected on the grounds of a large genetic component in intelligence. The genetic mechanism has been seriously misunderstood by those with little information about it. It is a leveler of human social classes from one generation to another. In each successive generation, it creates a new range of individual differences. High ability, by and large, dissipates more quickly from generation to generation than large fortunes.

The Nature-Nurture Issue

These nine generalizations are firmly established with the exception of the last. While there are no disconfirming data concerning black regression, the available data are not as broadly based as desirable. These nine generalizations do not constitute conclusive evidence for the genetic hypothesis, by any means. Alternative environmental hypotheses are possible, but these generalizations do restrict the nature of environmental hypotheses. Environmentalists must focus on development from conception to the beginning of the public-school period. This period includes several possible causes whose effects are irreversible. They must look for more subtle and more important causes than discrimination or lack of economic privilege. Most importantly, they must take a hard look at the problem and at superficial attempts to legislate psychological equality; the solution-by-slogan approach must be discarded. Indiscriminate use of the term *racist*, to describe any situation in which black and white outcomes differ, solves no problems.

"The very notion that a single general intelligence exists independent of environment is a peculiar one of doubtful validity."

Environment Helps Determine Intelligence

John Garcia

John Garcia earned his Ph.D. in psychology at the University of California, Berkeley. Raised on a fruit farm in northern California, he worked as a shipfitter and served four years in the Army during World War II before beginning his studies. While his main interests have been in the area of the biological constraints on learning, Mr. Garcia also has done research in social psychology and education. In the following viewpoint, he attempts to show why it is impossible to demonstrate, even with a scientifically controlled testing program, that general intelligence is inherited.

As you read, consider the following questions:

1. How does the author describe the story of Tryon's rat race?
2. What happens to IQ in the Israeli kibbutz, according to the author?

John Garcia, "I.Q.: The Conspiracy," *Psychology Today*, September 1972. Reprinted with permission of *Psychology Today*. Copyright © 1972 Ziff-Davis Publishing Company.

In 1929 at the University of California at Berkeley Robert C. Tryon set out to breed a race of intelligent rats. He needed a measure of the trait with which he was concerned. The rat crawled through a large automatic maze, hurried along by gates clicking closed behind it. Pressure plates on the maze floor made a record of the corridors it passed through. While all of Tryon's rats eventually found their way to the feeding pen at the exit, some consistently made more blind side excursions than others. Tryon bred his "bright" rats—the ones that went directly to the food—to each other, and did the same with his "dull" rats. About seven generations later Tryon was the owner of one thoroughbred line of bright rats, and one equally thoroughbred line of dull rats. But their brightness and dullness didn't mean much outside of Tryon's particular type of maze; the bright animals often did no better than the dull ones in tests in other learning situations. Tryon and other researchers began to suspect that the bright rats had scored high on Tryon's test because they were insensitive, undisturbed by clanking doors and switches. Other evidence suggested that the bright rats took the direct route because they were extremely food-oriented. Moreover, it appeared that the dull rats showed more caution and a more general tendency to explore than the bright rats. Both of these traits would be considered admirable and intelligent in other environments. To get a rat with a full spectrum of adaptive talents one probably should go to the city dump and trap one— the one that is hardest to catch.

The story of Tryon's rat race ends in vindicated truth; even a scientifically controlled breeding program based on an objectively measured test did not yield a rat general intelligence test or show the heritability of general intelligence....

The Meaning of IQ

The I.Q., or "intelligence" is a sort of social contract between educators and mental testers. The recent controversy on the relative intelligence of biosocial groups has given I.Q. a meaning and existence that ignore the very real limits on mental-measurement techniques: the designers of I.Q. tests built into them some intrinsic assumptions that make them useless for comparing the intelligence of biosocial groups. The use of I.Q. data for group comparisons changes the social contract into a social conspiracy to label particular groups inferior and to propagate the status quo. If we study the evolution of the I.Q. tests, these intrinsic assumptions— biases and limitations—become vividly apparent.

Our culture's most accepted, used, and standardized measure of "general intelligence" is the Stanford-Binet I.Q. test; Alfred Binet initiated the design in France between 1905 and 1911; Lewis Terman imported the project into the United States at Stanford University in 1916.

Robert Tryon was aware of some of the limitations of this testing.

In 1935 he pointed out that the idea of a single "general" intelligence depended on arbitrary assumptions made in the statistical procedures used to define intelligence factors. Different schools of psychometry can, and do, analyze the same test results into one, two, seven, or a virtually infinite number of more-or-less independent ability factors.

The number of intelligences emerging is a result of an arbitrary choice between viewing "more-or-less" independent abilities as "more" independent (treating them as distinct mental attributes), or as "less" independent (lumping them together).

A Middle-Class Instrument

An intelligence test is a middle-class white man's instrument, it is a device whites use to prove their capacities and get ahead in the white world. Achieving a high test score does not have the same meaning for a lower-status negro child, and it may even carry a definite connotation of personal threat. In this sense, scoring low on intelligence measures may for some talented negro children be a rational response to perceived danger.

Thomas F. Pettigrew, *A Profile of the American Negro*, 1964.

Binet built the test on the assumption of a single "general-intelligence" factor; this immediately affected the choice of individual items used for questions. Terman didn't want questions that would emphasize the more independent aspect of abilities; he did not want clusters of items—groups of questions in which getting one answer right would predict success on the other items of that group. He threw out items that formed clusters and kept questions that seemed to be independent of each other but that correlated well with the total score.

School Curriculum and "Anglos"

Except for this internal restriction, the designers were free to select questions from a myriad of types and sources. Terman restricted his choice to items from the school curriculum—worse yet, he picked only from those parts of the curriculum that school authorities deemed important: reading, writing, arithmetic. The traits manifested in Picasso's art, or those separating a master mechanic from a 10-thumbed apprentice, were pushed aside into the "specialized-abilities" category. If Terman had taken items from the machine shop, music class, art class, and other areas, concepts about what and whom to regard as intelligent might be broader than they are. Stanford-Binet I.Q. tests score "scholastic-performance intelligence," not "general intelligence."

The question of item sources was only the first of several problems that the testers handled with such pragmatic ingenuity. For the test to be useful, it had to have a standardization group—a reference group to determine what score is "normal," "high," or "low." The designers understood that the American school population at the turn of the century was a motley group, immigrants with a bewildering variety of ethnic, social and language backgrounds. But to insure validity in the standardization, it was necessary that the student understand the language and forms of the test questions. Accordingly, the testers included in the group only the children of white, English-speaking parents. The Stanford-Binet became an Anglo I.Q. test; it is hardly surprising that items based on common English usage are the most reliable subtest in it.

Coping with Age Differences

The psychometrists reached a third strategic landmark as they anticipated, detected, and resolutely suppressed the inelegant effects of the maturing of intellect; if older children are more successful than younger children on each test item, the raw score (number of correct answers) will show a nice, smooth increase with age. But many items do not behave this well. *A table is a thing. True or false?* might be a difficult question for a very young child. Children well into the school system would tend to get it right. A college philosophy student (or a precocious child) might consider a table to be a "concept" and mark the item false. The test designers eliminated any item that did not show a simple age-dependent performance improvement. Each time they narrowed the range of acceptable questions the concept of intelligence got smaller.

Age-change perturbations exist, in part because preschool children, schoolchildren, and postschool adults come from different biosocial strata. Five-year-old, 12-year-old, and 19-year-old girls are very different in biological attributes, and the cultural environments they live in change radically as they change in age....

The I.Q. test fails to measure general human intelligence for exactly the same reason that the Tryon maze cannot measure general rat intelligence. The test environment is far too narrow to emulate more than a sliver of the possible environments in which men and women find themselves....

The Israeli Kibbutz

The egalitarian structure of the Israeli kibbutz and the diversity of cultural background among members permit us to see what can happen to I.Q. if social factors are equalized. Outside the kibbutz in Israel, Jewish children of European parents have a mean I.Q. of 105, while a mean I.Q. of children of first-generation Oriental Jews is only 85. Some would suspect that the difference is genetic. When children of both groups grow up in the kibbutz nursery, after four years, they achieve exactly the same mean I.Q. scores—115 points. This does show us how labile I.Q. can be, but we should not conclude that the Oriental home inhibits intellect, or that the kibbutz environment stimulates it. It is far likelier that the Oriental home develops facets of intellect that are invisible to I.Q. tests, while the kibbutz makes a child test-wise.

A black child in a Northern city is not nearly as integrated into the test culture as the Oriental child in a kibbutz. He spends eight hours each day in a de-facto-segregated school and 16 hours in the black section of the city. An Oriental child in the kibbutz spends 22 hours a day in the nursery. The I.Q. of the black child usually does not reach the level of his Anglo urban counterpart. Chinese-Americans and Japanese-Americans score higher than Anglos do. None of this means much about inheritance of I.Q. Anglo scholastic I.Q. measured in a member of [a] non-Anglo biosocial group is a semimythical property. While I.Q. is only a tiny mental facet of the Anglo culture, it does have some biological reality if we use it only on Anglos. The heritability of I.Q. is higher in white persons than it is in black persons. This is not very odd: an Anglo I.Q. measured on a black person exists more on the psychometrist's score record than it does in the mind or brain of the black. Although the mind and brain will always manifest some effects of heredity, the psychometrist's score records are totally outside of genetic control.

Reflection of Social Environment

The very notion that a single general intelligence exists independent of environment is a peculiar one of doubtful validity and of no social utility. A person's performance on a mental test is always a reflection of the effect of social environment and the effect of his intrinsic mental attributes; these effects are inextricably fused in the test result. Mental tests sample the effects of social domains completely confounded with the effects of mental attributes. Social research and sophisticated statistics cannot tease apart these effects. When psychology fully recognizes this it can stop chasing its psychometric tail around empty questions and loaded answers.

"The weight of evidence is in favor of the proposition that racial differences in mental ability ...are innate and genetic."

IQ Tests Help Prove Intellectual Racial Differences

Henry E. Garrett

Henry E. Garrett taught at the University of Virginia, Charlottesville. He authored several books including *Great Experiments in Psychology, Testing for Teachers,* and *I.Q. and Racial Differences.* In the following viewpoint, the author argues that certain "racial" groups have mental abilities which are genetically inferior to those of others. To believe otherwise, he claims, is to fall prey to the "equalitarian dogma," a concept which he labeled "the scientific hoax of the century."

As you read, consider the following questions:

1. How does the author define the "equalitarian dogma"?
2. What evidence does the author give to support his idea that blacks are mentally inferior to whites?
3. According to the author, how are communists involved in the "equalitarian hoax"?
4. Do you agree with the author? Why or why not?

Henry E. Garrett, "The Equalitarian Dogma," *Perspectives in Biology,* Summer 1961. Reprinted by permission. © 1961 by The University of Chicago.

Up to World War I, it is probable that American scientists who gave the matter any thought at all believed the Negro race to be natively less gifted than the white. Thus, the Negro was generally considered to be less intelligent and more indolent than the white, and to be somewhat lacking in the fundamental traits of honesty and reliability. This judgement was concurred in by most white Americans.

Social scientists today do not often accept these onetime common-sense judgments. Instead, they hold that racial differences are skin deep: that whereas the black African differs from the white European in the breadth and depth of his civilization, there are no genetic or native factors to account for these differences; that all races are potentially equal in ability and differ only in their opportunity to achieve. Usually the social scientist will include motivation as a cause of racial differences, together with discrimination and prejudice.

The Equalitarian Dogma

This view that, except for environmental differences, all races are potentially equal has been called the *equalitarian dogma*. It has spread through many of our colleges and universities and is widely accepted by sincere humanitarians, social reformers, crusaders, sentimentalists, and (ostensibly) politicians. Many ministers of religion, convinced that the concept of the "equality of man" is in keeping with the ideals of Christian brotherhood and democracy, have joined the social scientists. Last, but by no means least, the Communists vigorously defend the equalitarian dogma. Only the man in the street, uninstructed in social anthropology, remains puzzled and reluctant.

Equalitarianism (or egalitarianism, as it is sometimes called) finds its chief support from at least two clearly identifiable sources: the allegedly scientific group who have "proved" equality, and the religious groups who accept this proof and, on the basis of it, assert that belief in racial differences implied "superiority" and "inferiority" and is unchristian, shameful, and blameworthy. Each camp supplements the other. The social scientists turn to moral denunciation when their evidence is feeble, and the religious fall back on "science" to bolster up their ethical preachments. From these two directions the American people have for more than thirty years been subjected to a barrage of propaganda unrivaled in its intensity and self-righteousness....

How can we account for today's shift from a general belief in native racial differences to acceptance of the equalitarian dogma? There are, I believe, five sources which have stimulated and directed the propaganda barrage mentioned above. Let us examine these in order.

By far the most potent assault upon native racial differences from the scientific side has come from the work of Franz Boas, who may be thought of as the "father" of the equalitarian movement. Boas came to this country from Germany in 1886 and for thirty-seven years (1899-1936) was professor of anthropology at Columbia University. Boas and his followers actively and aggressively championed equalitarianism, discounting any evidence tending to show that Negro-white differences may not be environmentally determined. But the cultural anthropologists rarely use objective measures recognized as valid for judging the comparative abilities of racial groups. Hence their conclusions, though confidently announced, are often subjective and unconvincing.

Bonuses for Sterilization

Bonuses would be offered for sterilization. Payers of income tax would get nothing. Bonuses for all others, regardless of sex, race, or welfare status, would depend on best scientific estimates of hereditary factors in disadvantages such as diabetes, epilepsy, heroin addiction, arthritis, etc. At a bonus rate of $1,000 for each point below 100 IQ, $30,000 put in trust for a 70 IQ moron potentially capable of producing 20 children might return $250,000 to taxpayers in reduced costs of mental retardation care. Ten per cent of the bonus in spot cash might put our national talent for entrepreneurship into action.

A feature that might frustrate the plan is that those who are not bright enough to learn of the bonus on their own are the ones most important to reach. The problem of reaching such people is what might be solved by paying the 10 per cent of the bonus in spot cash. Bounty hunters attracted by getting a cut of the bonus might then persuade low-IQ, high-bonus types to volunteer. I do not advocate the implementation of such a policy. But I do advocate objective inquiry.

William Shockley, *The Christian Century*, April 17, 1974.

The view presented here is that psychological tests offer the best—i.e., most valid—quantitative data for the determination of racial differences. The best recent survey of the comparative standing of American Negroes and American whites on a number of mental tests may be found in *Testing of Negro Intelligence*, a book written by A. M. Shuey, published in 1958. (It is indicative of the power—and lack of tolerance—of the equalitarians that none of the university presses to which this book was submitted was willing to publish it.) This book covers forty-four years, from 1913 to 1957, and analyzes some 240 studies. Negro-white comparisons are made of pre-school children, grade and high school pupils, college students, gifted and retarded children, soldiers, delinquents, racial hybrids, and Negro migrants. A brief summary of the relevant findings follows.

(1) I.Q.'s of American Negroes are from 15 to 20 points, on the

average, below those of American whites. (2) Negro overlap of white median I.Q.'s ranges from 10 to 25 per cent (equality would require 50 per cent). (3) About 6 times as many whites as Negroes fall in the "gifted child" category. (4) About 6 times as many Negroes as whites fall below 70 I.Q.—that is, in the feeble-minded group. (5) Negro-white differences in mean test score occur in all types of mental tests, but the Negro lag is greatest in tests of an abstract nature (for example, problems involving reasoning, deduction, comprehension). These are the functions called for in education above the lowest levels. (6) Differences between Negro and white children increase with chronological age, the gap in performance being largest at the high school and college levels. (7) Large and significant differences in favor of whites appear even when socioeconomic factors have been equated.

It seems clear that the evidence from psychometrics does not favor the equalitarian dogma; in fact, just the opposite.

Hitler and the Nazis

Undoubtedly Hitler's unspeakable cruelties and the absurd racial superiority theories of the Nazis set up a favorable climate for the proponents of the equalitarian dogma. It is easy for the equalitarian to argue that acceptance of the *fact* of racial differences is a forerunner of notions of racial superiority, discrimination, prejudice, and persecution. The argument is fallacious....

The Rise of African Nationalism

The struggle for freedom and self-determination by the various peoples of Africa has aroused the sympathy of most of the people of the world and has undoubtedly strengthened the emotional appeal in the idea that all men are born equally endowed. But emotionally founded beliefs can be deceptive. As is well known, the African Negro has been self-governing throughout most of his history, the colonial period being relatively short (only eighty years in the Belgian Congo). In the several thousand years of recorded history, the black African has never constructed an alphabet, created a literature or a science, produced any great men, or built up a civilization....

The Supreme Court Decision of 1954

In May of 1954, the Supreme Court of the United States handed down its decision on desegregation of the schools. This decree was hailed by proponents of the equalitarian dogma, who rightly regarded it as a great victory for their cause. Many people, however, were (and are) still confused by the issue of legal and moral rights and their relation to biological and psychological differences.

Undoubtedly the Communists (and their supporters) have aided in the spread and acceptance of the equalitarian dogma, although the extent and method of their aid is difficult to assess. Direct action

William Shockley and student protesters: Shockley's theories on genetics and IQ have been labeled as "racist" by many.

Wide World Photos

as well as subversion are both in the Communist creed. Communists have used equalitarian dogma as a device to gain converts among underprivileged people and also to foment trouble when possible. Many non-Communists hold the position that the free world must outdo the Communists in acceptance of this belief and must reject any further inquiry into its validity.

It will be apparent that in the writer's opinion the weight of evidence is in favor of the proposition that racial differences in mental ability (and perhaps also in character) are innate and genetic. The story is not finished, and further inquiry is sorely needed. Surely there are no scientific reasons why restrictions should be placed on further research. The equalitarian dogma, at best, represents a sincere if misguided effort to help the Negro by ignoring or even suppressing evidence of his mental and social immaturity. At worst, the equalitarian dogma is the scientific hoax of the century.

"IQ tests do not measure one's capacity to learn; a low score does not mean low ability."

IQ Tests Do Not Prove Intellectual Racial Differences

Robert L. Williams

Robert L. Williams received his Ph.D. in 1961 from Washington University in St. Louis. A founder of the Association of Black Psychologists, he served as chief psychologist of psychology service at St. Louis V.A. Hospital. When this viewpoint was written, Dr. Williams was director of black studies and professor of psychology at his alma mater, Washington University. In it, the author argues that IQ tests are simply one more racist tool used to help perpetuate the myth of white racial superiority. He offers evidence which he believes helps prove that IQ tests largely reflect one's cultural background, not innate intelligence.

As you read, consider the following questions:

1. What, according to the author, do IQ tests fail to measure? How does he define IQ?
2. What is a culture-specific intelligence test and how did the author use it?
3. Do you agree with the author? Why or why not?

The fundamental, inescapable problem for black people in America is still racism. The civil rights movement of the '60s focused on institutional racism, that oppressive cluster of laws, customs and practices that systematically supports doctrines of superiority and inferiority in America.

Now, blacks suffer another counterforce to survival: scientific racism. It has always been part of the American formula, but recently it has grown more virulent with advances in technology. This cold and inhumane experimentation with, and exclusion of, human beings is insidious because it is housed in universities, nurtured in industry, and cloaked in the language of rational science. An Ashanti proverb warns, "It is the calm and silent waters that drown a man." But the calmness fools no one; scientific racism is part of silent racial war, and the practitioners of it use intelligence tests as their hired guns.

I was almost one of the testing casualties. At 15, I earned an IQ test score of 82, three points above the track of the special education class. Based on this score, my counselor suggested that I take up bricklaying because I was "good with my hands." My low IQ, however, did not allow me to see that as desirable. I went to Philander Smith College anyway, graduating with honors, earned my master's degree at Wayne State University and my Ph.D. at Washington University in St. Louis. Other blacks, equally as qualified, have been wiped out.

The primary issues in the great black-white IQ controversy are not those of cultural test bias, the nature of intelligence, or the heritability of IQ. The issue is admittance to America's mainstream. IQ and achievement tests are nothing but updated versions of the old signs down South that read "For Whites Only." University admission policies have required standardized psychological tests such as the Scholastic Aptitude Test (SAT) or the Graduate Record Examination (GRE) as a criterion for admission to colleges, graduate schools, medical or law schools and other professional schools. For blacks, these tests more often mean exclusion....

Misconceptions About IQ

The educational institutions argue that testing is the fairest way to determine every child's ability. But no matter which argument one hears or believes, the results are the same. With few recent exceptions, black parents have had no control over whether or not their children were tested and how the test results would be used. Consequently, black children are placed, in disproportionate numbers, in classes for the mentally retarded, special-education classes or lower educational tracks.

Such misuse of psychological tests with black children is based upon several misconceptions. First, IQ cannot be inherited. An intelligence quotient (IQ) is nothing more than a score earned on a test. Actual intelligence covers a broad range of human abilities that

IQ tests do not even attempt to measure. For example, no test has formally assessed the many verbal and nonverbal skills required to survive in the black community. What we need is survival quotient (SQ), not an IQ.

Second, IQ tests do not measure the ability to succeed in the world, or even to get along in a different academic environment. Psychologists have designed these tests specifically to predict

---

Favored Status

Berkeley psychologist Arthur Jensen is back in the news again—this time with a new book [*Genetics and Education*] defending his thesis that blacks are genetically inferior to whites. Because of this, Jensen contends that it is folly to apply the same educational standards and techniques for white children to black children.

Four years ago, his article in the *Harvard Educational Review* on the topic stirred up a storm of controversy. His critics attacked his views as racist. He was picketed and barred from giving some scheduled lectures. Jensen has challenged his detractors to disprove his premise by coming up with some positive rebuttal based on research.

I agree with that point. His dogma is dangerous and frightening. Unless it is scientifically refuted, it will be around forever, haunting us. I propose that an impartial jury of eminent scientists and scholars in the field be empaneled to weigh all the evidence, pro and con, on the subject of genetic inferiority and come up with some conclusive findings.

I have a few questions to pose.

Number One: Does the Jensen theory confine itself to U.S. blacks alone? If not, does it apply also to the blacks of Africa and the Caribbeans, the island browns, the Asian yellows, and the other darker-hued peoples of the world?

Number Two: Considering the fact that American blacks have been diluted by an infusion of white blood through the slave-master relationship, which are the culprit genes that are responsible for the inferiority?

Number Three: How infallible are the methods by which Jensen arrived at his conclusions?

Let us put aside our emotions until the facts are sifted. We ought not to become involved in a brouhaha of name-calling and smear tactics. Meanwhile, Arthur Jensen might well begin probing the cause of the genetic disorders that lead the so-called master race to make war, pollute the air and the waters, defile the earth, perpetuate racial strife, and exploit the poor.

Ethel Payne, "Are Blacks Inferior?" *The Progressive*, June 1973. © 1973 CBS Inc. All rights reserved.

---

school success, but children must attend a school that adequately teaches the content of the test in order to score well. Most ghetto schools fail at this task.

A third misconception about the IQ test is its value as a measurement of mental retardation. Illiteracy is frequently equated with mental retardation, but literacy and intellect are not directly correlated. One who is highly literate is not necessarily a wise person or possessed of great intellect. Conversely, an illiterate person is not necessarily mentally retarded. Historical documents have shown that prior to the Civil War, masters often expropriated inventions from their uneducated black slaves. This act robbed the slaves of both their financial rewards and the intellectual credit due them.

Although lack of formal education and other obstacles excluded blacks from fields of science, many patented their inventions. Some of these, such as ice cream, potato chips, lawn mowers, and golf tees are in use today. One black man, Granville T. Woods, who received only a fifth-grade education, obtained about 50 patents, including one for the incubator.

Finally, IQ tests do not measure one's capacity to learn; a low score does not mean low ability. According to Bruno Bettelheim, "One boy who came to us diagnosed as feeble-minded today is a professor at Stanford."

Ebonics: The Oral Tradition

Many white researchers have claimed that black children are nonverbal and lack the ability to reason abstractly. There is irony in that view, since the culture of black people is based upon an oral tradition, dating back before Christ, that abounds in abstractions and symbolism. That tradition predates the Gutenberg press by at least 2,000 years. Proverbs, songs, prayers, myths, stories and legends were at the heart of formal and informal African educational systems.

Although the slave traders ripped the Africans from their native country, many of their customs and folkways survived the Atlantic passage. The slaves transplanted much of their oral traditions to the plantation, and incorporated them into black culture.

Blacks have maintained this African heritage, although Western chauvinism has isolated and belittled it as childlike and simpleminded. As Edmund Leach, the British anthropologist, has pointed out, the white Westerner is taught to believe that logical, mathematical, Aristotelian statements are the path to communication. This narrow perspective encourages reverence for literature and mathematics, and causes scorn for the metaphysical language of myth, which transcends logic. Westerners believe, says Leach, that they practice Aristotelian logic all the time. The truth is more complex, and consistent with the African tradition. Human beings communicate on many channels, with messages penetrating us through

BACK TO SCHOOL

Justus in the *Minneapolis Star*. Reprinted by permission.

our eyes, our ears, our noses, our skin. And communication between human beings is not complete without the nuances of tone of voice, gestures, shared visual perceptions and prior information held in common.

Black scholars are attempting to reconstruct the essence of the African tradition in a concept known as Ebonics. This concept combines linguistic and paralinguistic features that represent the communicative competence of West African, Caribbean and United

States slave descendants of African ancestors. It includes the various idioms, patois, argots, and social dialects of these regions. It also involves nonverbal cues, such as those referred to by Leach. Ebonics should not be confused with so-called Black English. The latter is a common hustle that was created, discussed and researched almost entirely by whites out of fascination with the ghetto. Black scholars have rejected the concept of Black English because it is simply poor grammer, and not uniquely black. Poor whites of the South speak the same English. Ebonics, unlike Black English, is different, not deficient.

Culture-Specific Testing

Given these differences in black culture, the rationale for a culture-specific intelligence test is clear. If a child can learn certain familiar relationships in his own culture, he can master similar concepts in the school curriculum, so long as the curriculum is related to his background experiences. For the average black child, there is too often a mismatching or discontinuity between the skills acquired from his culture and those required for successful test-taking and in the school curriculum.

L. Wendell Rivers, a black child psychologist and researcher, and I conducted a study to measure the effects of test instructions written in black dialectal language and in standard English on the performance of black children during intelligence testing. We divided 890 black kindergarten, first- and second-grade children into two groups of 445 each. We controlled for the variables of IQ, age, sex and grade in both the experimental and control groups. We used the standard version of the Boehm Test of Basic Concepts (BTBC), and a nonstandard version that we developed. The BTBC consists of 50 pictorial multiple-choice items involving concepts of space, quantity and time. Black teachers and graduate students translated the concepts and objects into the black idiom:

Standard Version	Nonstandard
Mark the toy that is *behind the sofa.*	Mark the toy that is *in back of the couch.*
Mark the apple that is *whole.*	Mark the apple that is *still all there.*
Mark the boy who is *beginning* to climb the tree.	**Mark the boy who is** *starting* **to climb the** tree. (Variation may be used as: about to, getting ready to.)

Children who took the test that was representative of their cultural background, i.e., the nonstandard version, scored significantly higher than the other group. The language of the standard version penalized the children taking the Boehm test.

That study suggested the need to develop a culture-specific test for black children. I conducted another experiment, this time using the Black Intelligence Test of Cultural Homogeneity (The BITCH Test) that I developed. I took 100 vocabulary items from the *Afro-American Slang* dictionary, my friends, and my personal experiences in working with black people. I gave the test to 100 black and 100 white subjects who were from 16 to 18 years old. Half in each group were from the low socioeconoimc level, and half were from the middle. The results showed that blacks scored much higher than whites on a test that was specific to their culture; the black subjects earned a mean score of 87.07, while the whites earned a mean score of 51.07. Clearly, if black children are given a culture-specific test that is representative of their backgrounds, they will do better than white children taking the same test.

Culture-Specific Tests for Blacks

The notion of a culture-specific test is not new. The Stanford-Binet, Wechsler Intelligence Scale for Children, and the Peabody Picture Vocabulary Test, among others, are clear examples of culturally specific tests. Representatives of the white middle-class culture contributed the bulk of the test items. White experts determined the correct responses, and all-white populations normalized them. Culture-specific tests for *black children* would only continue the tradition. The difference is that those children would not arrive in the classrooms of America with "unteachable" labels pasted, on the bias, to their permanent records.

Distinguishing Between Fact and Opinion

This activity is designed to help develop the basic reading and thinking skill of distinguishing between fact and opinion. Consider the following statement as an example: "The Wechsler Intelligence Scale is comprised of 11 different subtests." This statement is a fact. One need only look at the Wechsler Intelligence Scale to see that it is indeed made up of 11 subtests. But consider another statement about intelligence tests: "IQ tests are culturally loaded." As the variety of viewpoints in this chapter suggests, there is disagreement about whether IQ tests are culturally loaded. Hence this statement is an opinion.

When investigating controversial issues it is important that one be able to distinguish between statements of fact and statements of opinion. It is also important to recognize that not all statements of fact are true. They may appear to be true, but some are based on inaccurate or false information. For this activity, however, we are concerned with understanding the difference between those statements which appear to be factual and those which appear to be based primarily on opinion.

Most of the following statements are taken from the viewpoints in this chapter. Consider each statement carefully. *Mark O for any statement you believe is an opinion or interpretation of facts. Mark F for any statement you believe is a fact.*

If you are doing this activity as a member of a class or group, compare your answers with those of other class or group members. Be able to defend your answers. You may discover that others will come to different conclusions than you. Listening to the reasons others present for their answers may give you valuable insights in distinguishing between fact and opinion.

If you are reading this book alone, ask others if they agree with your answers. You too will find this interaction very valuable.

O = *opinion*
F = *fact*

132

1. The mean intelligence quotient of whites is 100.

2. Schools do not add to, let alone produce, the race difference.

3. Years ago, Southern schools for blacks were inferior in every way.

4. There was a major increase in education provided in America in the years following World War I.

5. In the survey by James Coleman in 1965, American Indians scored almost as high as Orientals in IQ tests.

6. Indians are more disadvantaged than blacks.

7. The differences between black and white cultures in America have been exaggerated.

8. A test standardized and validated on the white population is equally valid for blacks.

9. Eyeglasses correct a variety of inherited problems in vision.

10. Parents who have extreme scores in intelligence will have children, on the average, with less extreme scores than themselves.

11. The use of IQ tests is frequently not scientific at all.

12. Studies have shown that aptitude and intelligence tests frequently do not accurately predict a child's academic future.

13. From 1959 to 1963, nearly 1,700 black children in Prince Edward County, VA were denied schooling because of court-ordered desegregation.

14. Tests are tools which can be used wisely or harmfully, to help or hinder the educational growth of children.

15. At age 15, Robert Williams' IQ score was 82.

16. Educational testing can become an attack on black and poor children.

17. Intelligence tests have been based on a white, middle-class view of intelligence.

18. Low scores do not reflect general learning capabilities.

19. Intelligence tests predict equally well for blacks as for whites.

Bibliography

The following list of books and periodicals deals with the subject matter of this chapter.

Theodosius Dobzhansky and Ashley Montagu	"Natural Selection and the Mental Capacities of Mankind," *Science*, Vol. 105, 1947.
Ebony	"Mensa: The High IQ Society," October 1984.
Albert Einstein	*Out of My Later Years*. New York: Philosophical Library, 1950.
Howard Gardner	"Human Intelligence Isn't What We Think It Is," *U.S. News & World Report*, March 19, 1984.
Richard J. Herrnstein	"I.Q.," *The Atlantic Monthly*, September 1971.
Jeff Howard and Ray Hammond	"Rumors of Inferiority," *The New Republic*, September 9, 1985.
Jet	"Black Students Score Higher on SAT," April 2, 1984.
Frederick R. Lapides and David Burrows, eds.	*Racism: A Casebook*. New York: Thomas Y. Crowell Company, 1971.
Richard C. Lewontin	"Race and Intelligence," *Bulletin of the Atomic Scientists*, March 1970.
Kevin McKean	"Assault on the I.Q. Test," *Discover*, October 1985.
Scot Morris	"World's Hardest I.Q. Test," *Omni*, April 1985.
Anthony J. Motley	"The Educational Conspiracy: Exposed," *Lincoln Review*, Summer 1984.
National Review	"Wanted for Truth-Seeking; R.J. Herrnstein," July 8, 1973.
William Shockley	Playboy Interview, *Playboy*, August 1980.

Is Racial
Discrimination Prevalent?

Introduction

In 1964, following years of both peaceful and violent activities promoting racial equality, the Civil Rights Act was passed. It forbade discrimination in employment, housing, and a variety of other areas on the basis of race or sex. Court test cases, affirmative action programs, and measures such as forced school busing have all contributed to the official national position of racial equality. Yet today, the income of the average minority family remains less than two-thirds of that of the average white family while the unemployment rate for blacks and some other minorities is twice as high as that of whites. Is racism the cause of these discrepancies or are other factors involved?

The blatant racism of earlier eras—the separate "white" and "black" restrooms, drinking fountains, and seating sections in public places that were commonly found throughout the country only a few decades ago, for example—are no longer tolerated by the law. Many people, however, both minorities and white, argue that more subtle, though equally insidious, forms of racism persist today. The lack of strong, positive portrayals of minorities on television and in movies, the use of books in schools which perpetuate ethnic stereotypes, and the hiring of "token" minorities in visible but dead-end jobs are all examples to which these critics point.

On the other side are those who say that all of the legal mechanisms for equality are in place and now it is up to minorities to take advantage of the opportunities which have been made available. If minorities are behind in salaries or status, it is their own fault. Through hard work and assertiveness, these people say, members of minority groups can achieve as much as anyone else in society.

The viewpoints in this chapter debate the impact of racism on society today.

"The myth of steadily improving race relations is being dramatically exposed by the realities of the 1980s."

Racism Is Prevalent Today

Michael Omi and Howard Winant

Michael Omi, a teacher in the Asian American Studies Program at the University of California, Berkeley, and Howard Winant, a political sociologist, are editors of the bi-monthly journal *Socialist Review*. In the following viewpoint, they claim that while many improvements may seem to have been made, the United States is still a racist society. Further, they argue, the present trend toward conservatism underlines this undesirable fact.

As you read, consider the following questions:

1. List five examples the authors use to show that racism is present in US society today.
2. Mr. Omi and Mr. Winant list four specific ways the "new right" has re-introduced racism into American society. List and briefly explain them.
3. The authors write that racism today is more subtle than the overt racism of the past but just as insidious. What are some of the ways they claim today's racists justify their bigotry?

Michael Omi and Howard Winant, "By the Rivers of Babylon: Race in the United States," *Socialist Review*, September/October 1983, 3202 Adeline St. Berkeley, CA 94703. Reprinted with permission.

The myth of steadily improving race relations is being dramatically exposed by the realities of the 1980s. Both mainstream politics and sensational events have underscored the emergence of a "new racism." On a number of fronts the Reagan administration has attempted to roll back the progressive gains of minorities secured over the last several decades. It has reversed the federal government's already tenuous positions on busing and affirmative action and exhumed the notorious "states' rights" slogan. In addition, it has made unsuccessful bids to block the renewal of the Voting Rights Act and extend federal tax breaks to schools that discriminate against people of color.

The rightward drift of the country as a whole has fostered a "politics of resentment." The expansion of racial minority rights has been seen as "bending over backward" to appease minority demands. Whites are now seen as a disadvantaged majority. Last year, the Association for White Students at Southern Methodist University in Dallas, Texas, became an official student organization with the expressed goal to "promote equality by ending reverse discrimination."

In minority communities fear abounds as a virtual epidemic of racially motivated violence finds among its victims random children, joggers, and the head of the Urban League. But perhaps the most visible warning that a new period of intensified racial conflict has begun is the presence throughout the nation of various orders of the Ku Klux Klan. From the shooting deaths of Communist Workers Party members in Greensboro, North Carolina, to the violent harassment of Vietnamese shrimpers in Texas, to electoral bids in California, Michigan, and North Carolina, the headlines suggest that the Klan is alive, well, and, unfortunately, growing.

Racial Politics

More ominous than these more "visible" expressions of racism is the manner in which political discourse increasingly relies on a *racial understanding* by which to comprehend domestic and international issues.

—The current influx of immigrants and refugees from Mexico, Cambodia, Vietnam, Haiti, and Cuba, among other countries, has been met in a climate of scarcity with "fear and loathing" by many Americans. Rising unemployment, scarce housing, and state cutbacks have contributed to a demand for restriction, if not outright exclusion, of immigration on grounds implicitly shaped by racial criteria. A repressive new immigration law, the Simpson-Mazzoli bill, with bipartisan and administrative support is currently being approved.

—Domestic economic woes are blamed on unfair foreign competition—with Japan receiving an inordinate amount of responsibility. National polls show an increase in unfavorable attitudes

138

toward Japan, and Asian Americans are beginning to feel the brunt of this shift in climate. Last year in Detroit, a Chinese American man was beaten to death by a laid-off auto plant foreman and his stepson who mistook their victim for Japanese and blamed him for the loss of their jobs.

—The decline of the American empire, epitomized by the "losses" of Vietnam, Nicaragua, and Iran, has led to a renaissance of national chauvinism. Revived nationalism in the United States contains important ideological elements which view the geo-political alignments in racial terms.

—Racial conflict is not confined to the white/nonwhite color line. The battle lines have been redrawn as demographic changes and the impoverishing effects of stagflation have exacerbated tensions among racial minorities. In many regions, whites have remained relatively shielded from conflict as Latinos and Asians collide over housing in Denver and blacks and Southeast Asian immigrants fight over social service benefits in San Francisco.

Racism Harms American Indians

The American sin of racism has wounded American Indians. The United States Commission on Civil Rights stated in its 1981 publication, *Indian Tribes, A Continuing Quest for Survival:* "This racism has served to justify a view not repudiated, but which lingers in the public mind, that Indians are not entitled to the same legal rights as others in this country....At one extreme the concept of inferior status of Indians was used to justify genocide; at the other, apparently benevolent side, the attempt was to assimilate them into the dominant society. Whatever the rationale or motive, whether rooted in voluntary efforts or coercion, the common denominator has been the belief that Indian society is an inferior lifestyle."

Ted Zuern, *America*, May 28, 1983.

Racial conflict and the very meaning of race itself are becoming central political issues in the 1980s. The many newly emerging patterns of racial conflict will differ significantly from those which the nation has experienced in the past. The confrontations and reforms of the 1950s and 1960s altered the manner in which racism had operated, but these transformations were not far-reaching enough to prevent the subsequent reintroduction of various new forms of racism throughout the social fabric....

Racial Restructuring

Since the early 1970s, a reactive restructuring of the American racial order has been in progress; this process affects all major institutions and interacts with every political issue, even those such as sex/gender, nuclear power, or gun control, which seemingly have no "direct" relationship to patterns of racial oppression....

In many respects the reconstituion of racial oppression in the United States is an ideological process. The contemporary right has demonstrated this....Some of the major currents in the rearticulation process as practiced by the new right are:

1. *Anti-statism and fiscal resentment:* The state is seen as operating at the expense of the middle strata who pay the taxes and finance social-welfare programs. State activity is understood as a drain on the "free market"; hence state workers and especially benefit recipients are attacked as parasites....Tax-revolt initiatives such as California's Proposition 13 and Massachusetts' Proposition 2½ flow readily from these sentiments.

Traditional (Racist) Morality

2. *Reassertion of "traditional morality":* Nearly all of the so-called "social issues" being pushed by the Moral Majority and the Conservative Caucus contain significant racial elements. There is also an important zone of overlap between some of these racial themes and sex/gender-oriented elements animated by homophobia and anti-feminism. Stigmatization of single-parent- (that is, female-) headed households, opposition to abortion, antagonism to gun control, demands for "law and order" at the expense of civil liberties and judicial independence, reassertion of militaristic and jingoistic themes (e.g., opposition to the Panama Canal treaty signed by Carter, Reagan's claim that the Vietnam War was a "noble cause") furnish ready examples. Coded phrases such as "defense of the family," "getting government off our backs," "the permissive society," and, perhaps most familiar, "reverse discrimination" are employed in racial (and sexual) discourse which does not need to make explicit reference to race.

In the relatively few instances where race is explicitly considered by new-right spokespersons, the results are quite grotesque:

> What actually happened since 1964 was a vast expansion of the welfare rolls that halted in its tracks an ongoing improvement in the lives of the poor, particularly blacks, and left behind—and here I choose my words as carefully as I can—a wreckage of broken lives and families worse than the aftermath of slavery. Although intact black families are doing better than ever, and discrimination has vastly diminished, the condition of poor blacks has radically worsened. The fact that they have more income only makes the situation less remediable. [George Gilder, *Wealth and Poverty.*]

This is the theory employed to justify vast programmatic shifts in domestic policy. Rearticulation processes are particularly evident here: Gilder's laissez-faire attitude links race, sex, and class themes in a repressive moralistic doctrine.

3. *Economic initiatives adversely affecting racial minorities:* Buoyed up by such new-right "thought," two categories of economic policy

damaging to racial minorities have been pursued by the Reagan forces....

"Cutbacks" has become a familiar term indeed in minority communities, where it is not difficult to recognize the racial dimensions of an economic program designed to reduce inflation by increasing unemployment and by eliminating (as far as possible) those social expenditures that bring income and consumption goods into the ghetto/barrio. From the standpoint of the various minority communities, there is little contradiction between the two points of the Reaganomics lance. In fact, in certain respects the two approaches appear mutually reinforcing. The free-marketeers assault the community straightforwardly, withdrawing badly needed services and jobs as unemployment climbs. The supply-siders offer half-baked schemes: subsidies (tax-based) to corporations to locate "free enterprise zones" in the ghetto/barrio. In other words residents are "whitemailed" into accepting inferior jobs at substandard pay, with no safety standards or prospects of improvement, precisely because services and publicly funded employment have been withdrawn.

"Spatial Deconcentration"

Further initiatives adversely affecting minority communities are proposals for dispersing the ghetto and barrio populations (so-called "spatial deconcentration") as gentrification of inner-city areas prices housing out of the reach of most minority-group residents; elimination of busing and any commitment to school integration, a process well under way as public education continues to be systematically underfunded; neglect of the "frostbelt" cities and "sunset" industries, where large numbers of minority populations and workers are concentrated, and continuing emphasis on military expenditures, which employ far fewer minority workers than do other forms of public outlay.

Individualism as Racist

4. *Opposition to "group rights" and reassertion of individualism:* With affirmative action the new right has advanced the farthest in its efforts to rearticulate the discourse of the movement for racial equality. Its opposition to those demands embodies a harsh new "common sense" centered on the charge of "reverse discrimination," which is linked in turn to long-standing anti-egalitarian traditions. This phrase takes the commitment to equal opportunity presented by the civil-rights movement and embeds it in a new conservative discourse which appeals to principles of individual merit in the allocation of scarce resources.

The defection rightward of an important group of liberal intellectuals—the "neoconservatives"—has provided the main mouthpieces for the attack on the "group rights" demand embodied in the principle of affirmative action. Nathan Glazer, one of the leading neoconservatives, argued in 1975 for the reinstate-

141

ment of individually oriented and "color-blind" anti-discrimination policies, and thus for an end to affirmative action. According to Glazer, affirmative action

> has meant that we abandon the first principle of a liberal society, that the individual and the individual's interests and good and welfare are the test of a good society, for we now attach benefits and penalties to individuals simply on the basis of their race, color, and national origins. The implications of this new course are increasing consciousness of the significance of group membership, an increasing divisiveness on the basis of race, color, and national origin, and a spreading resentment among the disfavored groups against the favored ones. If the individual is the measure, however, our public concern is with the individual's capacity to work out an individual fate by means of education, work and self-realization in the various spheres of life. Then how the figures add up on the basis of whatever measures of group we use may be interesting, but should be of no concern to public policy....

Covert Racism

It is a measure of the progress against racism that it is more difficult today for the racists to propagate and peddle their wares openly and in the old crude ways. This is the positive side. But in some ways, it is more difficult to fight racism that is camouflaged, racism that is attached as a rider to other complex issues....

Concerning racism in federal programs, it should not matter what the race or national mix of those benefiting from them is. The food stamp program is an example. What should matter is that people who need food stamps are all poor and hungry. But in its drive to get support for cutting food stamps, the Reaganites use a racist pitch. By implication they put over the idea that white Americans should not protest these cuts because they only affect Black, Puerto Rican and Chicano people.

This maneuver cuts two ways. It spreads racism and cuts socio-economic programs. It covers up the fact that more whites will be cut off food stamps than Afro-Americans or other oppressed national minorities. Even the cuts in funds for housing are put over with the racist subterfuge that housing is only a ghetto problem....

On all these questions, and more, racism is slipped in as a rider. The intent is to create confusion and divisions, to promote prejudice and warped biases. The purpose is to keep working and poor people from seeing their common interest, as well as their common enemy.

Gus Hall, *Daily World*, February 28, 1985.

Neoconservative opposition to affirmative action, and the effort to label it "reverse discrimination" (or in Glazer's case, "affirmative discrimination"), epitomizes the commitment to redefine racial meanings in such a way as to contain the more radical implications of the minority movements that preceded it. Racial discrimination, and racial oppression in general, are to be understood—in the neoconservative lexicon—as problems to be confronted on an individual level. They are illegitimate infringements on individual rights, but they are not legitimate sources for group demands....

In Summary

Unable to justify racial oppression in the aftermath of [the civil rights movement,] the most sustained assault on [racism] since the Civil War, the new right has sought to restrict its meaning to discrimination against individuals and overtly manifested racial prejudice. Appeals to traditional elements of morality ("you can't change human nature"), to the necessity of controlling inflation, and to the "demeaning" and "debilitating" character of public expenditure for the ghetto/barrio (as in the case of Gilder), all operate to rearticulate racial meanings in individual terms.

Turbulence will continue to characterize race relations in the coming years. Race relations will be deeply embedded in the overall crisis of American politics.

"Over the years intergroup relations have been changing for the better, and...positive changes have been accumulating, with little backsliding."

Racism Is No Longer Prevalent

Philip Perlmutter and Walter E. Williams

Philip Perlmutter, the author of Part I of the following viewpoint, is a writer whose articles appear frequently in the Boston *Globe*, the *Christian Science Monitor, Commentary,* and other publications. Walter E. Williams, the author of Part II, is a professor of economics at George Mason University and an adjunct scholar of The Heritage Foundation. In the following viewpoint, the authors argue that too little credence is given to the progress that's been made toward eradicating racism. Mr. Perlmutter states that social critics tend to "prove" racism's influence through faulty reasoning. Professor Williams writes that problems attributed to racism often have other logical explanations.

As you read, consider the following questions:

1. Mr. Perlmutter lists six fallacies in the way social critics often assess society's attitudes toward race. List these fallacies and tell in your own words what each means.
2. Mr. Williams cites several examples he claims black leaders use to show that blacks are the victims of discrimination. Why does Mr. Williams believe these examples are misleading?

Philip Perlmutter, "Fallacies of Evaluation," *The Lincoln Review*, Winter 1985. Reprinted with permission.

Walter E. Williams, "Black 'Leaders' Tell Only Part of the Story," *Human Events*, January 10, 1981. Reprinted by permission of *Human Events*.

I

In any discussion of prejudice and discrimination, two questions inevitably arise over facts and values. One is whether or not America was or is democratic or undemocratic, racist or free, and, as if to gain a more reasoned answer, the adverbs "really" or "truly" are added. Qualified or not, the question attempts to assess the facts as they were or are.

The second question attempts to evaluate the situation over a period of time. Have conditions been improving or getting worse since the writing of the Bill of Rights, the 14th Amendment, the 1954 Supreme Court desegregation decision, Martin Luther King Jr.'s 1963 March on Washington, the War on Poverty, or any president's term of office. Here, too, for added emphasis, "really" or "truly" is inserted to affirm or challenge the evaluation. While only a foolish few would try to deny the existence of intergroup hostility, an equally foolish few would argue an absence of improvement.

The justification for a positive or negative assessment is usually laden with passion, ideology, politics—and, at times, historical ignorance. Nevertheless, the questions are appropriate, for they reflect a profound concern about basic values, beliefs and ideals.

Improved Race Relations

All too often in recent years, the answers have been in the negative, regardless of who was President, with intergroup relations projected as bad or never worse, and as if any admission of societal well-being or progress was tantamount to being uncaring or callous to existing social ills. Such assessments are not only inaccurate, but work against solving the very problems deplored. They fail to recognize that over the years intergroup relations have been changing for the better, and that positive changes have been accumulating, with little backsliding.

Such meliorism is usually scorned, particularly by those who believe America a racist or a well-intentioned nation heading towards two separate and unequal societies. Such people—whether reformers or revolutionaries—commit a number of perceptual, philosophical, logical and historical fallacies:

First is that of selective perception, wherein only injustices are seen or reported and improvements ignored. Thus, it is commonplace for many minority leaders to espouse solutions to bigotry, which can vary with what most members of their group believe. For example, while increasing numbers of "minority" leaders have called for "quotas," polls have consistently shown minority group members opposing them.

For example, as far back as 1977, at least 80 percent of women and 55 percent of Blacks preferred "ability" to "preferential treatment." Five years later, a broad range of ethnic groups believed that ability based on test scores should be the main consideration for

145

jobs and college entrances: Poles by 81.5 percent; Italians, 80 percent; Irish, 77.5 percent; Jews, 76 percent; and Hispanics, 60.5 percent. In 1983, 77.7 percent of whites and 52.2 percent of non-whites polled believed companies should hire "the most qualified person," while only 15.3 percent of whites and 40.7 percent of non-whites believed companies should be legally required to hire a certain percentage of minority group members, even if not the most qualified. Similarly, an early 1984 Gallup poll revealed that women, too, chose "ability" over "preferential treatment" in "getting jobs and places in college" by 84 percent to 11 percent—and non-whites did so by 64 percent to 27 percent.

Busing Issue Transcends Racism

Similarly, though outright racists have opposed school busing (forced or voluntary), so have a majority of people of both races:

—A 1976 Harris poll showed that 51 percent of the Blacks and 81 percent of the whites did so, and in another poll, 52 percent of the Blacks and 75 percent of the whites believed "busing school children across district lines makes relations between the races worse."

Cries of "Racism" Undermine Minorities

The dangers of the present course are both insidious and acute. Among the insidious dangers are the undermining of minority and female self-confidence by incessant reiteration of the themes of pervasive discrimination, hypocritical standards and shadowy but malign enemies relentlessly opposing their progress. However successful this vision may be in creating a sense of dependence on "civil rights" and "women's liberation" movements, it also obscures the urgency of acquiring economically meaningful skills or developing the attitudes to apply them with the best results.

Thomas Sowell, *Civil Rights: Rhetoric or Reality?* 1984.

—A 1981 *Newsweek* poll of black opinion revealed half of the respondents agreeing that school busing "caused more difficulties than it is worth." Similarly, a *New York Times*/CBS News Poll found that 45 percent of the Blacks polled opposed school busing for racial integration, while only 37 percent favored it. Even in some cities where busing had been introduced, Black opposition increased. For example, before busing began in 1977 in Wilmington, Delaware, 40 percent of the Black parents opposed it, but a year later, the percentage rose to 50 percent, though there had been no violence or picketing by whites. Some Black leaders, like Derrick A. Bell Jr., who had represented the NAACP in over 300 school desegregation cases, now claimed that the equating of "racially balanced schools with the right to an equal education opportunity is a certain formula for losing both" and that integrated schools did not bring about "either interracial understanding or academic improvement for poor black children."

—In 1982, polls revealed broad ethnic opposition to busing for improving school racial balance: Irish, 79.5 percent; Italian, 79 percent; Polish, 74 percent; Jewish, 68 percent; and Hispanic, 50.5 percent.

That Was Then; This Is Now

A second fallacy is that of vestigial observation, wherein present-day symptoms or charges of bigotry are confused with yesteryears' actual diseases. Any college or industry which does not admit or hire a particular minority group member or set percentage is vulnerable to vilification for bigotry, though the greater truth is that more minorities than ever before are entering schools and obtaining jobs. Gone are the virulent anti-Japanese, anti-Chinese, anti-Catholic or anti-Semitic behaviors of past decades and centuries. The reality of the day is that groups once excluded are now included, and that with increasing frequency, it is done on a preferential basis.

Another fallacy is that of petrified language. Though the deplored situation may have changed or disappeared, the language description remains and is applied to a different situation. Thus, any unequal pay for women is referred to as "sexism," or any brutality against a minority member is labelled "genocide," or any criticism of a minority is rejected as "anti-Semitism," or "racism." Simply put, every example or alleged example of inequality, brutality or criticism is not group oppression, genocide or racism. Ironically, rather than "discrimination" being defined as invidious treatment because of race, sex, religion or national origin, it has come to mean absence of favorable treatment because of such factors.

Fourth is the fallacy of indiscriminate comparisons, where a group is criticized or condemned for not being like "our" group—or "our" group is hailed because it is not like *that* one. No or little thought is given to the sociological factors which contributed to differences between "we" and "they," nor is there any historical recognition that today's non-discriminated against groups were once so targetted. History shows that nothing said about today's Black, Asian or Hispanic groups was not said about yesteryear's Irish, Italian, Greek, Polish, Jewish, or Scotch-Irish immigrants.

Prejudice Can't Explain All Differences

Pseudo-egalitarianism is a fifth fallacy, wherein all people and groups are considered fundamentally alike and that if only everyone were treated equally, no differences would exist and intergroup harmony would prevail. Existing differences in learning, income, educational achievement, or social behavior are credited, or blamed, or living in privileged circumstances or a hostile environ-

147

ment. Such reasoning invariably ignores that within and between groups some people work harder or do not want to work harder than others, save or spend more, have larger or smaller families, prefer certain games and pastimes, and are not equally motivated by nature or nurture to obtain the same goals in life.

Pride in Progress

Racism or radical intolerance has been mankind's most frequent companion throughout history. No place on Earth has escaped one sort or another of racial strife. Despite the lofty words of our Declaration of Independence and Constitution, Americans failed to avoid this ugly fellow-traveler.

What makes us unique is *not* a history of racial intolerance, but a history of having done something about it. Our Constitution, which once provided little if any protection to blacks, proved to be the strongest weapon in the civil rights struggle. That struggle is now over; moreover, civil rights have won, and we can be proud....

The surest sign that the civil rights struggle is over lies in the new causes taken by civil rights "leaders" who don't want to be unemployed. Jesse Jackson goes around praising tyrants like Fidel Castro and Yasser Arafat, and trying to organize farmers.

Walter Williams, *The Washington Times*, June 14, 1985.

Prejudice and discrimination alone can never explain why some groups succeed in rising to higher socio-economic and educational levels than other groups, as in the cases of Jews, Chinese, Japanese, Irish, Armenians, Huguenots and Mormons—or why some groups have more family members working or not working. Also at work are differential age levels in high-level jobs, which are usually reached at the age of 40 or 50. For example, the Mexican American and Puerto Rican average age is below twenty, that of Irish Americans and Italian Americans is over thirty, and that of Jews is over forty. Thus, gaining experience and obtaining good jobs is intricately related to getting older, so that minority group representation in high level jobs cannot be compared to representation in a population that includes many five-year olds—yet it is.

In education, too, some minorities have higher percentages of young people. While nearly one-third of all white Americans are 19 years old or under, it is 40 percent for all Blacks and Hispanics, who represent close to 30 percent of the nation's high school student body, though comprising 20 percent of the total population. In 1983, approximately 50 percent of all Black and 60 percent of all Hispanic households had children of school age—in contrast to less than 40 percent of white households.

The last fallacy is that of "doomsday" generalization, which foresees a group's eventual extinction because of historic and immutable bigotry. Thus, the Jewish Defense League and the early Black Panthers saw another holocaust or genocide in the making because of latent or blatant examples of anti-Semitism or racism, though both were at their lowest levels—attitudinally and behaviorally. Similarly, there are millenialists—religious and political—who await an imminent "end of days" or world revolution, which, as of this writing, has not occurred.

How shall groups be evaluated? Certainly not as above—and certainly not in absolute or politically partisan concepts, which distort the potentiality and actuality of group existence and progress.

II

Somebody should tell the emperor that he has no clothes on.

For years now, black "leaders" have been pretending that all the problems of black people can be attributed to white racism. Libraries, bookshelves and newspaper offices are crammed with tomes explaining what black people are, what they think, why they have problems, and what government can do to lead them out of the wilderness. Much of this material is now considered sacred. To question it—or worse, to criticize it—leaves one open to harsh attack. If he is lucky, the critic may be called an insensitive clod, or perhaps a political reactionary. If he's less fortunate, he'll be called a racist, or in the case of a black, an Uncle Tom.

Vernon Jordan, president of the National Urban League, has been quoted as equating blacks with the boat people. After paying their dues to American society for all of these years, he said, they are no better off.

Economic Differences Natural

While it is not unfashionable to question the statement of a black leader, someone might have asked Mr. Jordan how such a characterization jibes with income statistics. The average black family outside the South which has both husband and wife working earns about the same as a young white family.

True, median income for black people as a whole is slightly lower than that of whites, because this group is younger than most other ethnic groups in the U.S. The median age for blacks is 22 years, while that of Polish-Americans is 40 years and that of Italians is 36, to choose two other groups.

Suppose we had a world where no racial discrimination existed; wouldn't you still expect median income to differ between ethnic groups? Of course it would, if their median ages varied.

What about black leaders who protest that blacks are being victimized and brutalized by police? This statement, put in its proper perspective, borders on the insane. I am not about to pretend that no acts of brutality are ever committed by police. But most of the violence committed in the black community cannot be blamed on either the police or on white people. If you don't believe me, just go to the Bronx or to Harlem or to North Philadelphia and ask black people, huddled in their homes at night in fear, *whom* they fear. I doubt whether they will say police authorities or white people.

Crime Not Fault of Racism

Already I can hear some self-appointed expert on crime in the black community saying, "Perhaps—but it is racism in the larger society that is responsible for blacks turning on blacks." Nonsense. When I was a kid growing up in the 1940s, on hot nights black people would often sleep on rooftops, fire escapes and doorsteps to escape the oven-like condition of their apartments. I'm sure if a black person did that today, his marbles would be counted. Surely there was more racial discrimination in the 1940s, yet black people had greater safety in their persons and property.

Blacks Can Make It on Their Own

Americans have trouble digesting the notion that the country owes a particular group something. The case is more difficult to make when there is double-digit unemployment and many middle-class families, regardless of race, have difficulties making ends meet. It would be difficult to design a better strategy to serve racists and demagogues than one that postulates that blacks require and reserve special, even preferential treatment. Millions of qualified blacks reject the implication that they cannot make it on their own without special help....

Blacks as a group do not want hand-outs or special treatment. Black dignity may well have been the biggest loser when this country's ethic of individualism was threatened. The restoration of that dignity will surely be the greatest dividend a re-evaluation of compensatory treatment could bring to blacks and the nation.

Haskell G. Ward, *The New York Times*, June 29, 1985.

Blame for the current state of affairs, in reality, lies in the tolerance of the court toward criminals and in the support that black leadership gives to the criminal element of the black community. I would like to see black politicians and ministers, instead of calling a news conference to condemn the police shooting of a black criminal, call a news conference to demand better protection for women raped and mugged, for people who have their homes broken into on a regular basis, and for the poor people who buy paint to fix up their homes, only to have them defaced again by graffiti.

Benjamin Hooks, chairman of the NAACP, recently lamented the fact that whites in America no longer feel guilty about past treatment of blacks.

I've been wanting for years to give whites "reparation certificates" for both their own grievances and those of their forebears against my people. Maybe then, white people could stop feeling guilty and acting like fools and start treating black people just like they treat white people. Because if they didn't feel guilty, they wouldn't approve the teaching of "black English" in some of our schools. The English spoken by many black youngsters does not originate in black culture or history; it represents a failure of the school system. Black English is new. Talk to someone in his 60s, 50s, or even younger, and see whether you hear this dialect. Or better yet, talk to Hooks, Jordan or any of our black congressmen—people who have "made it" in the white man's world.

Guilt Felt by Whites

Guilt felt by many whites has led them to support programs and many forms of behavior that they would not tolerate if displayed by whites. This, I believe, is one of the most insidious forms of racism.

I urge: Be brave. If a black does a job that's inferior or makes statements that ignore the facts, hold him accountable. If he does a job that's superb or speaks insightfully, tell him so. All the evidence that I have shows that black people are strong and they can take it—whatever criticism or commendation that you have to give.

"There is no such thing as good racial discrimination."

Affirmative Action Is Racist

Charles Murray

Charles Murray is Senior Research Fellow at the Manhattan Institute for Policy Research. The author of the controversial book, *Losing Gound: American Social Policy 1950-1980*, Mr. Murray believes that all governmental social programs actually hurt, rather than help, the people at which they are aimed. In the following viewpoint, he argues that affirmative action is just a dressed-up form of racism. It encourages people to think of blacks differently than whites because of their race.

As you read, consider the following questions:

1. How is every black professional "tainted" by affirmative action, according to the author?
2. What does the author believe would happen if affirmative action was eliminated?
3. How does the author believe affirmative action perpetuates the idea of black inferiority?

Charles Murray, "Affirmative Racism," *The New Republic*, December 31, 1984.
Reprinted by permission of THE NEW REPUBLIC, © 1985, The New Republic, Inc.

A new racism...is emerging to take its place alongside the old. It grows out of preferential treatment for blacks, and it is not just the much-publicized reactions, for example, of the white policemen or firemen who are passed over for promotion because of an affirmative action court order. The new racism that is potentially most damaging is located among the white elites—educated, affluent, and occupying the positions in education, business, and government from which this country is run. It currently focuses on blacks; whether it will eventually extend to include Hispanics and other minorities remains to be seen.

The new racists do not think blacks are inferior. They are typically longtime supporters of civil rights. But they exhibit the classic behavioral symptom of racism: they treat blacks differently from whites, because of their race. The results can be as concretely bad and unjust as any that the old racism produces. Sometimes the effect is that blacks are refused an education they otherwise could have gotten. Sometimes blacks are shunted into dead-end jobs. Always, blacks are denied the right to compete as equals.

The new racists also exhibit another characteristic of racism: they *think* about blacks differently from the way they think about whites. Their global view of blacks and civil rights is impeccable. Blacks must be enabled to achieve full equality. They are still unequal, through no fault of their own (it is the fault of racism, it is the fault of inadequate opportunity, it is the legacy of history). But the new racists' local view is that the blacks they run across professionally are not, on the average, up to the white standard. Among the new racists, lawyers have gotten used to the idea that the brief a black colleague turns in will be a little less well-rehearsed and argued than the one they would have done. Businessmen expect that a black colleague will not read a balance sheet as subtly as they do. Teachers expect black students to wind up toward the bottom of the class.

The new racists also tend to think of blacks as a commodity. The office must have a sufficient supply of blacks, who must be treated with special delicacy. The personnel problems this creates are more difficult than most because whites barely admit to themselves what's going on....

Black Academic Performance

When American universities embarked on policies of preferential admissions by race,.....they had good reason to be optimistic that preferential treatment would work—for many years, the best universities had been weighting the test scores of applicants from small-town public schools when they were compared against those of applicants from the top private schools, and had been giving special breaks to students from distant states to ensure geographic distribution. The differences in preparation tended to even out after the first year or so. Blacks were being brought into a long-standing

153

and successful tradition of preferential treatment.

In the case of blacks, however, preferential treatment ran up against a large black-white gap in academic performance combined with ambitious goals for proportional representation. This gap has been the hardest for whites to confront. But though it is not necessary or even plausible to believe that such differences are innate, it is necessary to recognize openly that the differences exist. By pretending they don't, we begin the process whereby both the real differences and the racial factor are exaggerated....

As universities scramble to make sure they are admitting enough blacks, the results feed the new racism. Here's how it works:

In 1983, only 66 black students nationwide scored above 700 in the verbal section of the Scholastic Aptitude Test, and only 205 scored above 700 in the mathematics section. This handful of students cannot begin to meet the demand for blacks with such scores. For example, Harvard, Yale and Princeton have in recent years been bringing an aggregate of about 270 blacks into each entering class. If the black students entering these schools had the same distribution of scores as that of the freshman class as a whole, then every black student in the nation with a verbal score in the 700s, and roughly 70 percent of the ones with a math score in the 700s, would be in their freshman classes.

Quotas Discriminate

Call them goals, quotas, ratios (or what you will), the fact remains that any such numerical device that prefers some over others for racial reasons is outlawed discrimination....

To label such preferential treatment *"affirmative* action" insults common intelligence.

William Bradford Reynolds, *Human Events*, November 30, 1985.

The main problem is not that a few schools monopolize the very top black applicants, but that these same schools have much larger implicit quotas than they can fill with those applicants. They fill out the rest with the next students in line—students who would not have gotten into these schools if they were not black, who otherwise would have been showing up in the classrooms of the nation's less glamorous colleges and universities. But the size of the black pool does not expand appreciably at the next levels. The number of blacks scoring in the 600s on the math section in 1983, for example, was 1,531. Meanwhile, 31,704 nonblack students in 1983 scored in the 700s on the math section and 121,640 scored in the 600s. The prestige schools cannot begin to absorb these numbers of other highly qualified freshmen, and they are perforce spread widely throughout the system.

At schools that draw most broadly from the student population, such as the large state universities, the effects of this skimming produce a situation that confirms the old racists in everything they want most to believe. There are plenty of outstanding students in such student bodies (at the University of Colorado, for example, 6 percent of the freshmen in 1981 had math scores in the 700s and 28 percent had scores in the 600s), but the skimming process combined with the very small raw numbers means that almost none of them are black. What students and instructors see in their day-to-day experience in the classroom is a disproportionate number of blacks who are below the white average, relatively few blacks who are at the white average, and virtually none who are in the first rank. The image that the white student carries away is that blacks are less able than whites.

Characteristics of New Racism

I am not exalting the SAT as an infallible measure of academic ability, or pointing to test scores to try to convince anyone that blacks are performing below the level of whites. I am simply using them to explain what instructors and students already notice, and talk about, among themselves.

They do not talk openly about such matters. One characteristic of the new racism is that whites deny in public but acknowledge in private that there are significant differences in black and white academic performance. Another is that they dismiss the importance of tests when black scores are at issue, blaming cultural bias and saying that test scores are not good predictors of college performance. At the same time, they watch anxiously over their own children's test scores....

The same process continues in graduate school. Indeed, because there are even fewer blacks in graduate schools than in undergraduate schools, the pressures to get black students through to the degree, no matter what, can be still greater. But apart from differences in preparation and ability that have accumulated by the end of schooling, the process whereby we foster the appearance of black inferiority continues....

Black and White Abilities

The pool of black candidates for any given profession is a small fraction of the white pool. This works out to a 20-to-1 edge in business; it is even greater in most of the other professions. The result, when many hiring institutions are competing, is that a major gap between the abilities of new black and white employees in any given workplace is highly likely. Everyone needs to hire a few blacks, and the edge that "being black" confers in the hiring decision warps the sequence of hiring in such a way that a scarce resource (the blacks with a given set of qualifications) is exhausted at an artificially high rate, producing a widening gap in comparison with the remaining whites from which an employer can choose.

The more aggressively affirmative action is enforced, the greater the imbalance. In general, the first companies to hire can pursue strategies that minimize or even eliminate the difference in ability between the new black and white employees. IBM and Park Avenue law firms can do very well, just as Harvard does quite well in attracting the top black students. But the more effectively they pursue these strategies, the more quickly they strip the population of the best black candidates....

New Racism Excludes Blacks

Even if a black is hired under terms that put him on a par with his white peers, the subtler forms of differential treatment work against him. Particularly for any corporation that does business with the government, the new employee has a specific, immediate value purely because he is black. There are a variety of requirements to be met and rituals to be observed for which a black face is helpful. These have very little to do with the long-term career interests of the new employee; on the contrary, they often lead to a dead end as head of the minority-relations section of the personnel department.

Added to this is another problem that has nothing to do with the government. When the old racism was at fault (as it often still is),

Bob Dix, *Manchester Union Leader*. Reprinted with permission.

the newly hired black employee was excluded from the socialization process because the whites did not want him to become part of the group. When the new racism is at fault, it is because many whites are embarrassed to treat black employees as badly as they are willing to treat whites. Hence another reason that whites get on-the-job training that blacks do not: much of the early training of an employee is intertwined with menial assignments and mild hazing. Blacks who are put through these routines often see themselves as racially abused (and when a black is involved, old-racist responses may well have crept in). But even if the black is not unhappy about the process, the whites are afraid that he is, and so protect him from it. There are many variations, all having the same effect: the black is denied an apprenticeship that the white has no way of escaping. Without serving the apprenticeship, there is no way of becoming part of the team....

Every Black Tainted

The most obvious consequence of preferential treatment is that every black professional, no matter how able, is tainted. Every black who is hired by a white-run organization that hires blacks preferentially has to put up with the knowledge that many of his co-workers believe he was hired because of his race; and he has to put up with the suspicion in his own mind that they might be right.

Whites are curiously reluctant to consider this a real problem—it is an abstraction, I am told, much less important than the problem that blacks face in getting a job in the first place. But black professionals talk about it, and they tell stories of mental breakdowns; of people who had to leave the job altogether; of long-term professional paralysis. What white would want to be put in such a situation? Of course it would be a constant humiliation to be resented by some of your co-workers and condescended to by others. Of course it would affect your perceptions of yourself and your self-confidence. No system that produces such side effects—as preferential treatment *must* do—can be defended unless it is producing some extremely important benefits.

What About the Future?

And that brings us to the decisive question. If the alternative were no job at all, as it was for so many blacks for so long, the resentment and condescension are part of the price of getting blacks into the positions they deserve. But is that the alternative today? If the institutions of this country were left to their own devices now, to what extent would they refuse to admit, hire, and promote people because they were black? To what extent are American institutions kept from being racist by the government's intervention?

It is another one of those questions that are seldom investigated aggressively, and I have no evidence. Let me suggest a hypothesis that bears looking into: that the signal event in the struggle for black equality during the last thirty years, the one with real impact, was not the Civil Rights Act of 1964 or Executive Order 11246 or any other governmental act. It was the civil rights movement itself. It raised to a pitch of acute and lasting discomfort the racial consciousness of the generations of white Americans who are now running the country. I will not argue that the old racism is dead at any level of society. I will argue, however, that in the typical corporation or in the typical admissions office, there is an abiding desire to be not-racist. This need not be construed as brotherly love. Guilt will do as well. But the civil rights movement did its job. I suggest that the laws and the court decisions and the continuing intellectual respectability behind preferential treatment are not holding many doors open to qualified blacks that would otherwise be closed.

Racism Required

One of the biggest open secrets of American life is the widespread use of reverse discrimination, including overt racial and sexual preferences and quotas, for the distribution of jobs, school admissions, and other scarce positional goodies. How this came about, despite a prevailing ideology opposing overt group favoritism, is a great saga of legal sophistry, resulting in a system that theoretically forbids reverse discrimination while actually requiring it in almost all walks of life.

Michael Kinsley, *Harper's*, June 1983.

Suppose for a moment that I am right. Suppose that, for practical purposes, racism would not get in the way of blacks if preferential treatment were abandoned. How, in my optimistic view, would the world look different?

Fewer Blacks at Harvard and Yale

There would be fewer blacks at Harvard and Yale; but they would all be fully competitive with the whites who were there. White students at the state university would encounter a cross-section of blacks who span the full range of ability, including the top level, just as whites do. College remedial courses would no longer be disproportionately black. Whites rejected by the school they wanted would quit assuming they were kept out because a less-qualified black was admitted in their place. Blacks in big corporations would no longer be shunted off to personnel-relations positions, but would be left on the main-line tracks toward becoming comptrollers and sales managers and chief executive officers. Whites would quit assuming that black colleagues had been hired because they were black. Blacks would quit worrying that they had been hired because they were black.

Would blacks still lag behind? As a population, yes, for a time, and the nation should be mounting a far more effective program to improve elementary and secondary education for blacks than it has mounted in the last few decades. But in years past virtually every ethnic group in America has at one time or another lagged behind as a population, and has eventually caught up. In the process of catching up, the ones who breached the barriers were evidence of the success of that group. Now blacks who breach the barriers tend to be seen as evidence of the inferiority of that group.

The Evil of Affirmative Action

And that is the evil of preferential treatment. It perpetuates an impression of inferiority. The system segments whites and blacks who come in contact with each other so as to maximize the likelihood that whites have the advantage in experience and ability. The system then encourages both whites and blacks to behave in ways that create self-fulfilling prophecies even when no real differences exist.

It is here that the new racism links up with the old. The old racism has always openly held that blacks are permanently less competent than whites. The new racism tacitly accepts that, in the course of overcoming the legacy of the old racism, blacks are temporarily less competent than whites. It is an extremely fine distinction. As time goes on, fine distinctions tend to be lost. Preferential treatment is providing persuasive evidence for the old racists, and we can already hear it *sotto voce:* "We gave you your chance, we let you educate them and push them into jobs they couldn't have gotten on their own and coddle them every way you could. And see: they still aren't as good as whites, and you are beginning to admit it yourselves." Sooner or later this message is going to be heard by a white elite that needs to excuse its failure to achieve black equality.

The only happy aspect of the new racism is that the corrective—to get rid of the policies encouraging preferential treatment—is so natural. Deliberate preferential treatment by race has sat as uneasily with America's equal-opportunity ideal during the post-1965 period as it did during the days of legalized segregation. We had to construct tortuous rationalizations when we permitted blacks to be kept on the back of the bus—and the rationalizations to justify sending blacks to the head of the line have been just as tortuous. Both kinds of rationalization say that sometimes it is all right to treat people of different races in different ways. For years, we have instinctively sensed this was wrong in principle but intellectualized our support for it as an expedient. I submit that our instincts were right. There is no such thing as good racial discrimination.

"In choosing a qualified applicant because of a race preference we merely acknowledge ...'the burdens, stigmas, and scars produced by history...the injustices heaped on his ancestors.'"

Affirmative Action Is Not Racist

Herman Schwartz

Affirmative action was first instituted by the federal government to actively seek out minorities and others who suffered from the effects of discrimination and to give them an opportunity at equal education and job opportunities. Whether it actually has accomplished this is a source of contention. In the following viewpoint, Herman Schwartz argues that affirmative action has resulted in advancing blacks, and believes attacks on affirmative action are unfounded. Mr. Schwartz is a professor of law at American University in Washington, DC and is director of the William O. Douglas Inquiry into the State of Individual Freedom.

As you read, consider the following questions:

1. Does the author believe that racism is prevalent today?
2. What example does the author give to support his argument that affirmative action works?
3. The author asserts that discrimination in employment occurs everyday. Do you think this is true?

The attack on affirmative action is only a small part of [the Reagan] administration's campaign against the hard-won rights of blacks, women, and other groups that suffer the inequities of society. Since 1964 this country has developed and refined a body of constitutional, statutory, and regulatory approaches designed to exorcise the existence and effects of the racism and sexism so deeply entrenched in our society. Until 1981 all of our presidents, to a greater or lesser extent, contributed to this effort, even when, like Richard Nixon, they were less than enthusiastic....

Affirmative action has been defined [by Myrl Duncan] as "a public or private program designed to equalize hiring and admission opportunities for historically disadvantaged groups by taking into consideration those very characteristics which have been used to deny them equal treatment." The controversy swirls primarily around the use of numerical goals and timetables for hiring or promotion, for university admissions, and for other benefits. It is fueled by the powerful strain of individualism that runs through American history and belief.

Undoing Racism and Sexism

It is a hard issue, about which reasonable people can differ. Insofar as affirmative action is designed to compensate the disadvantaged for past racism, sexism, and other discrimination, many understandably believe that today's majority should not have to pay for their ancestors' sins. But somehow we must undo the cruel consequences of the racism and sexism that still plague us, both for the sake of the victims and to end the enormous human waste that costs society so much. Civil Rights Commission Chairman Pendleton has conceded that discrimination is not only still with us but is, as he put it, "rampant." [In] January 1984, the dean of faculty at Amherst College wrote in the *New York Times:*

> In my contacts with a considerable range of academic institutions, I have become aware of pervasive residues of racism and sexism, even among those whose intentions and conscious beliefs are entirely nondiscriminatory. Indeed, I believe most of us are afflicted with such residues. Beyond the wrongs of the past are the wrongs of the present. Most discriminatory habits in academia are non-actionable; affirmative action goals are our only instrument for focusing sustained attention.

The plight of black America not only remains grave, but in many respects, it is getting worse. The black unemployment rate—21 percent in early 1983—is double that for whites and the gap continues to increase. For black 20- to 24-year-old males, the rate—an awful 30 percent—is almost triple that for whites; for black teenagers the rate approaches 50 percent. More than half of all black children under three years of age live in homes below the poverty line. The gap between white and black family income, which prior to the '70s had narrowed a bit, has steadily edged wider, so that black-family income is now only 55 percent of that of whites. Only 3 percent of the nation's lawyers and doctors are black and only 4 percent of its managers, but over 50 percent of its maids and garbage collectors. Black life expectancy is about six years less than that of whites; the black infant mortality rate is nearly double....

Division by Race and Gender

We must close these gaps so that we do not remain two nations, divided by race and gender. Although no one strategy can overcome the results of centuries of inequity, the use of goals and timetables in hiring and other benefit distribution programs has helped to make modest improvements. Studies in 1983 show, for example, that from 1974 to 1980 minority employment with employers subject to federal affirmative action requirements rose 20 percent, almost twice the increase elsewhere. Employment of women by covered contractors rose 15 percent, but only 2 percent among others. The number of black police officers nationwide rose from 24,000 in 1970 to 43,500 in 1980; that kind of increase in Detroit produced a sharp decline in citizen hostility toward the police and a concomitant increase in police efficiency. There were also large jumps in minority and female employment among firefighters, and sheet metal and electrical workers.

Color Consciousness a Necessity

A pernicious history of slavery and segregation has embedded discriminatory patterns into our social and economic fabric. These pervasive patterns cause seemingly neutral or color-blind operations of our society to be inherently prejudicial.

Corporations' "old boy" networks, particularly, build on years of friendship and social contact cultivated at predominantly white, all-male preparatory schools and colleges. Recruiting for jobs is often done by word of mouth. Information is exchanged and corporate strategies devised in clubs whose membership is confined to white males and whose dues are often paid by employers....

To overcome entrenched discriminatory patterns that infect our society, the Supreme Court again and again has confirmed the constitutional appropriateness of color-conscious remedies.

Murray Saltzman, *The New York Times*, June 28, 1983.

Few other remedies work as well or as quickly. As the New York City Corporation Counsel told the Supreme Court in the *Fullilove* case about the construction industry (before Mayor Edward Koch decided that affirmative action was an "abomination"), "less drastic means of attempting to eradicate and remedy discrimination have been attempted repeatedly and continuously over the past decade and a half. They have all failed.''

What, then, is the basis for the assault on affirmative action?

Apart from the obvious political expediency and ideological reflex of this administration's unvarying conclusion that the ''haves'' deserve government help and the ''have-nots'' don't, President Reagan and his allies present two related arguments: (1) hiring and other distributional decisions should be made solely on the basis of individual merit; (2) racial preferences are always evil....

Quoting Dr. Martin Luther King, Jr., Thurgood Marshall, and Roy Wilkins to support the claim that anything other than total race neutrality is ''discriminatory,'' Assistant Attorney General [William Bradford] Reynolds warns that race consciousness will ''creat[e]...a racial spoils system in America,'' ''stifle the creative spirit,'' erect artificial barriers, and divide the society. It is, he says, unconstitutional, unlawful, and immoral.

Midge Decter, writing in the *Wall Street Journal*....sympathized with black and female beneficiaries of affirmative action programs for the ''self-doubts'' and loss of ''self-regard'' that she is sure they suffer, ''spiritually speaking,'' for their ''unearned special privileges.''

Destroying Sense of Self

Whenever we take race into account to hand out benefits, declares Linda Chavez, the new executive director of the Reagan Civil Rights Commission, we ''discriminate,'' ''destroy[ing] the sense of self.''

The legal position was stated by Morris Abram....

> I do not need any further study of a principle that comes from the basic bedrock of the Constitution, in which the words say that every person in the land shall be entitled to the equal protection of the law. Equal means equal. Equal does not mean you have separate lists of blacks and whites for promotion, any more than you have separate accommodations for blacks and whites for eating. Nothing will ultimately divide a society more than this kind of preference and this kind of reverse discrimination.

In short, any form of race preference is equivalent to racism.

All of this represents a nadir of ''Newspeak,'' all too appropriate for this administration....For it has not only persistently fought to curtail minority and women's rights in many contexts, but it has used ''separate lists'' based on color, sex, and ethnic origin whenever politically or otherwise useful....

Does Affirmative Action Discriminate?

But what of the morality of affirmative action? Does it amount to discrimination? Is it true, as Brian Weber's lawyer argued before the Supreme Court, that ''you can't avoid discrimination by discriminating''?...Were Martin Luther King, Jr., Thurgood Marshall, Roy Wilkins, and other black leaders against it?

Hardly. Indeed, it is hard to contain one's outrage at this perversion of what Dr. King, Justice Marshall, and others have said, at this manipulation of their often sorrow-laden eloquence, in order to deny a handful of jobs, school admissions, and other necessities for a decent life to a few disadvantaged blacks out of the many who still suffer from discrimination and would have few opportunities otherwise.

No one can honestly equate a remedial preference for a disadvantaged (and qualified) minority member with the brutality inflicted on blacks and other minorities by Jim Crow laws and practices. The preference may take away some benefits from some white men, but none of them is being beaten, lynched, denied the right to use a bathroom, a place to sleep or eat, being forced to take the dirtiest jobs or denied any work at all, forced to attend dilapidated and mind-killing schools, subjected to brutally unequal justice, or stigmatized as an inferior being.

Enforcing Constructive Change

Affirmative action is the means of constructive change. With it, we can continue to open doors to those long denied the opportunity to compete. The executive order should be affirmed. The door should not be closed.

Ralph P. Davidson, *The New York Times*, November 25, 1985.

Setting aside, after proof of discrimination, a few places a year for qualified minorities out of hundreds and perhaps thousands of employees, as in the Kaiser plant in the *Weber* case, or 16 medical-school places out of 100 as in *Bakke*, or 10 percent of federal public work contracts as in *Fullilove*, or even 50 percent of new hires for a few years as in some employment cases—this has nothing in common with the racism that was inflicted on helpless minorities, and it is a shameful insult to the memory of the tragic victims to lump together the two....

Troubling Questions Raised

Does affirmative action divide people? Is group thinking immoral? Dangerous? Where does it stop—aren't we all minorities, and aren't we all therefore entitled? If so, won't we wind up with claims totaling 200 percent of the pie? Should a white policeman or fire fighter with ten years in the department be laid off when a black or a woman with less seniority is kept because an affirmative action decree is in force? Aren't those denied a job or another opportunity because of an affirmative action program often innocent of any wrong against the preferred group and just as much in need of the opportunities?

The last question is the most troubling. Brian Weber was not a rich man and he had to support a family on a modest salary, just like any black worker. A craft job would have been a significant step up in money, status, and working conditions. And *he* hadn't discriminated against anyone. Why should he pay for Kaiser's wrongs?

Few Whites Adversely Affected

A closer look at the *Weber* case brings some other factors to light. Even if there had been no separate list for blacks, Weber would not have gotten the position, for there were too many other whites ahead of him anyway. Moreover, but for the affirmative action plan, there would not have been any craft training program at the plant at all, for *any* whites.

Furthermore, even with the separate list, the number of whites adversely affected was really very small. The Kaiser plan (adopted "voluntarily" to avoid employment discrimination suits by blacks and the loss of federal contracts) contemplated hiring only three to four minority members a year, out of a craft work force of 275-300 and a total work force of thousands. In the first year of its operation, Kaiser still selected only a handful of blacks, because it also brought in 22 outside craftsmen, of whom only one was black. In the 1980 *Fullilove* case, in which the Supreme Court upheld a 10 percent set-aside of federal public works projects for minority contractors, only 0.25 percent of the total annual expenditure for construction in the United States was involved. In *Bakke*, only 16 places out of 100 at one medical school were set aside for minorities. A new Boston University special admissions program for black medical students will start with three a year, with the hope of rising to ten, increasing the minority enrollment at the school by 2 percent.

The *Weber* case discloses another interesting aspect of affirmative action plans. Because they can adversely affect the careers of majority white males, creative ingenuity is often expended to prevent this from happening. In *Weber*, a new craft program benefiting both whites and blacks was set up. Although white employees and the union had been clamoring for such a program for many years, it wasn't until Kaiser felt it had to adopt an affirmative action program that it granted this request. In the lay-off cases, time sharing and other ways of avoiding the dismissals—including raising more money—can be devised. So much for Mr. Reynold's worries about "stifling the creative spirit."

Strains can and do result, especially if deliberately stirred up. But strain is not inevitable: broad-ranging goals and timetable programs for women and blacks were instituted in the Bell Telephone Company with no such troubles. The same holds true elsewhere, especially when, as in *Weber*, the program creates new, previously unavailable opportunities for whites. On the other hand, some whites may be upset, even if...the remedies are limited to specific identifiable victims of discriminatory practices. If a black applicant can prove that an employer wrongly discriminated against him personally, he would be entitled to the seniority and other benefits that he would have had but for the discrimination...and this would give him competitive seniority over some white employees regardless of those employees' innocence. The same thing happens constantly with veterans' and other preferences, and few opponents of affirmative action seem to be upset by that.

Justice, Not Discrimination

To say that breaking up the white male monopolies is discrimination against the monopolizers is both illogical and hypocritical. It is true that some white males will have to sacrifice in this process of just redistribution, but sacrifice is the price of justice in the social order. Social justice may in times of war require sacrifice, even to the point of death. Affirmative action, fortunately, does not require that, but the sacrifice that it does require is a matter of justice, not of discrimination.

Daniel C. Maguire, *USA Today*, July 1981.

Among some Jews, affirmative action brings up bitter memories of ceiling quotas, which kept them out of schools and jobs that could on merit have been theirs. This has produced a serious and nasty split within the civil rights movement. But affirmative action goals and timetables are really quite different. Whereas quotas against Jews, Catholics, and others were ceilings to limit and keep these groups out of schools and jobs, today's "benign preferences" are designed to be floors that let minorities into a few places they would not ordinarily enter, and with relatively little impact on others.

Aren't We All Minorities?

There is also a major confusion, exploited by opponents, resulting from the fact that we are almost all ethnic or religious minorities. Of course we are. And if it were shown that any minority is being victimized by intentional discrimination *and* that the only way to get more of that minority into a relatively representative portion of the work force or school is through an affirmative action plan, then these people would be entitled to such a remedy.

There is really nothing inherently wrong about taking group identity into account, so long as the person selected is qualified, a prerequisite that is an essential element of all affirmative action programs. We do it all the time, with hardly a murmur of protest from anyone. We take group identity into account when we put together political slates, when a university gives preference to applicants

166

from a certain part of the country or to the children of alumni, when Brandeis University restricts itself to Jews in choosing a president... or Notre Dame to Roman Catholics or Howard University to blacks, when we give preference to veterans for jobs, promotions, and the like....Some of these examples are less laudable than others. But surely none of these seldom criticized practices can be valued above, or has the serious purpose of undoing, the effects of past and present discrimination. In choosing a qualified applicant because of a race preference we merely acknowledge, as Morton Horwitz has pointed out, "the burdens, stigmas, and scars produced by history...the injustices heaped on his ancestors and, through them on him. The history and culture of oppression, transmitted through legally anonymous generations, is made antiseptic when each individual is treated as a separate being, disconnected from history."

Importance of Ethnic Diversity

In some cases, moreover, group-oriented choices are necessary for effective performance of the job. Justice Powell in the *Bakke* case noted the importance of ethnic and other diversity for a university, as a justification for taking race into account as one factor in medical school admissions. He did stress that the choice must be individualized, but his choice of the Harvard program as a model gave away the ball game because a key part of it (described in the appendix to his opinion but not in the excerpt he chose to quote) is a certain number of minority admissions as a goal.

One area where effective job performance almost mandates such group consideration is...police departments. The confrontation of an almost all-white police force with an angry, socially depressed minority community has produced violence, police brutality...,and inefficient police work. Those unhappy conditions were in fact a major reason for extending Title VII of the Civil Rights Act to state and local governments.

Such race-conscious selection within police departments has worked. In Detroit, a largely black city where racial friction between a nearly all-white police force and ghetto dissidents had been epidemic and bloody—one such incident sparked the violence in 1968 that led to the death of 34 people—the police department voluntarily instituted an affirmative action plan that, as the Justice Department itself has admitted, "was expressly made as a response to undeniable past discrimination against blacks that had created a police force that was largely unresponsive to the concerns of a substantial portion of the City's population." Since then racial incidents and police/community frictions have declined....

Solving Problems

Affirmative action has, of course, not always been completely effective. No policy can be. Certain marginally qualified students have been unable to meet the academic demands of colleges and professional schools. Once these problems emerged, however, many schools set up special remedial programs that, like the Kaiser craft training plan, often benefited needy whites as well....

The seniority layoff problem is undeniably the most troubling, for in this case people lose jobs they *have*, obviously a more serious matter than not getting a job you want but don't have. But layoffs on the traditional "last in, first out" basis will undo what little progress we have made toward racial equity. And a layoff of whites is far more likely to result in quick rehiring than a layoff of blacks, as Boston and Memphis both showed: when the courts in those cases ordered whites to be laid off, money suddenly materialized and all the laid-off workers were promptly rehired....

A Tradition Without a Past

"Equal is equal" proclaims Morris Abram, and that's certainly true. But it is just as true that equal treatment of unequals perpetuates and aggravates inequality. And gross inequality is what we still have today. As William Coleman, secretary of transportation in the Ford administration, put it,

> For black Americans, racial equality is a tradition without a past. Perhaps, one day America will be color-blind. It takes an extraordinary ignorance of actual life in America today to believe that day has come....[For blacks], there is another American "tradition"—one of slavery, segregation, bigotry, and injustice.

"Any book that leads a teacher to openly discriminate and to offend a student should be seriously questioned for its appropriateness as a tool of instruction."

'Huckleberry Finn' Is a Racist Novel

Margot Allen

Margot Allen is a black parent whose childhood memories of studying *Huckleberry Finn* were filled with racial discrimination. When her young son was similarly offended a generation later, she began a campaign to eliminate the book from the school' curriculum. She is the academic coordinator for Penn State University's Office of Academic Assistance Program. In the following viewpoint, she cites the reasons why she believes that racist books should be removed from classrooms.

As you read, consider the following questions:

1. What, according to the author, are the racist elements in *Huckleberry Finn*?
2. How did the son's English teacher justify her actions when teaching the book?
3. What actions did the author take to prevent *Huckleberry Finn* from being taught? Was she successful?

Margot Allen, "Huck Finn: Two Generations of Pain." Reprinted by permission of the Council on Interracial Books for Children, 1841 Broadway, New York, NY 10023 from the Council's *Bulletin*, Vol. 15, No. 5. A free catalog of the Council's print and audiovisual materials is available.

My adventure with *Huckleberry Finn* has been a stinging and bitter one, one which has left a dull pain that spans two generations, mine and my son's.

Today, during the book's centenary, while Mark Twain specialists and scholars laud this book as one of the "most profound, most transcendent literary images the human imagination has ever come up with," it is easy for me to recall a time nearly 30 years ago, a time that seemed like an eternity of teeth-clenching and inner contortions that threatened to betray my extreme discomfort when reading this book in the ninth grade. Had I shared my tension and stress with my teacher or classmates, I would have literally frightened them, and my Blackness would have stood out even more than it did as I read the book along with everyone else and kept my feelings in check.

But such negative experiences with *Huck Finn* are not a thing of the past. Just three years ago, when my son was thirteen, he too was victimized by those same negative images. I am sharing our story with you now in the hopes that teachers, school administrators and parents will be more sensitive to the negative racial elements of this book and will begin to question, research and speak out regarding how and when this book can best be taught.

My story begins with two different classroom experiences some 30 years apart. In both accounts I focus on feelings and reactions because I believe these represent the very foundation upon which most complaints about the book rest. They are personal but real, and to ignore these feelings, to intellectualize them or to misconstrue them as an excuse to charge censorship, would be to continue with a status quo that oppresses people of color. We need to come to grips with *Huck Finn's* powerful imagery and the *feelings* evoked by those images.

An Introduction to *Huck*

I was first introduced to *Huck Finn* in 1957. I was thirteen and in the ninth grade of a large, middle-class, suburban, predominantly white high school in Portland, Oregon. I was the only Black student in the class. When *Huck Finn* was assigned, there was no advance preparation; we simply started to read the book, a classic whose name held a familiar—and friendly—ring for most students. As we began to get into the story, however, the dialect alone made me feel uneasy. And as we continued, I began to be apprehensive, to fear being singled out, being put on the spot, being ridiculed or made fun of because of my color, and only because of my color! It was the exact same feeling I'd had as a child when a supposedly "fun game" turned into a hurting one. The feelings that I had as a ninth grader reading *Huck Finn* very much resembled those that I had as a child playing "eenie, meenie, minie, moe: catch a ____ by the toe." While it never occurred to me to refuse to play such games, I would pray like the dickens that no one would use that awful word—the very word my parents had taught me was used only by people who were ignorant or of low moral character. And there it was, in print, that word, staring me in the face over and over again throughout the entire book.

I need not tell you that I hated the book! Yet, while we read it, I pretended that it didn't bother me. I hid, from my teacher and my classmates, the tension, discomfort and hurt I would feel every time I heard that word or watched the class laugh at Jim and felt some white youngster's stare being directed my way, as if to say, "Hey, it's you and your kind we're talking about in this book." I think the hardest part was keeping my composure while being stared at. Somehow I thought that a blank face would protect me from not only this book's offensiveness and open insults, but the silent indicting, accusing and sometimes apologetic stares of my classmates. After all, the very last thing I wanted anyone to think was that I was ashamed of being Black, even though I could not identify with Jim or other Blacks in the novel.

Inflicting Pain on Black Children

Being Black, I remember vividly the experience of having read *Huck Finn* in a predominantly white junior high school in Philadelphia some 30 years ago. I can still recall the anger and pain I felt as my white classmates read aloud the word "nigger." In fact, as I write...I am getting angry all over again....

Why should a learning experience, intended to make children love literature, instead end up inflicting pain upon Black children?

Bulletin, vol. 15, nos. 1/2, 1984.

I suffered silently through the reading of *Huck Finn*; at times, I attempted to fake a certain easiness with the book that I thought my classmates had. I learned very little from this experience about literature, the antebellum South or slavery. I learned precious little, if anything, about the novel as a form and the elements of irony and satire.

A Generation Later

I was so glad to move on to something else that I completely suppressed the experience (a not uncommon experience for Black people)—until my son ran into *Huck Finn* in his English class three years ago. (*Huck Finn* was one of the core books in the ninth-grade English curriculum of the State College Area Intermediate High School in State College, Pa., a small college town that is, incidentally, the home of Penn State University.) My son, the only Black youngster in his class, was asked by his teacher to read the part of Jim aloud. When a curious white youngster immediately asked why he was selected, the teacher replied, "He has the perfect voice for it." At that, the class laughed. My son was humiliated, though he, too, tried to hide his feelings, just as I had so many years before. After class a number of his friends came up to him and made comments like, "Gee, I'm sorry, the teacher's a real jerk." Others were not so supportive. One child said, "That must tell you what the teacher thinks of you," and there were those who took the opportunity to snicker "nigger" under their breath to him.

Greatly distressed by my son's experience, I called the Vice-Principal who, in turn, had the teacher call me later that same morning. In our discussion, I asked why she chose my son to read Jim's part and told her emphatically that I did not want him to read that part. The teacher reported that in years past, whenever she had Black students in her class, she'd asked them to read Jim's part and without exception, they had been "proud" to do so. (She also said that she felt that since slavery was a part of the black heritage, my son should be proud to authenticate that history by reading Jim's part aloud...and after all, since he is Black, he could read the part better than the white students.)

Use of *Huck Finn* Questioned

Incensed by this teacher's lack of sensitivity and understanding, I wrote to the State College Area Intermediate High School asking that *Huck Finn* be immediately discontinued as required reading. I felt that any book that leads a teacher to openly discriminate and to offend a student should be seriously questioned for its appropriateness as a tool of instruction. I also questioned the real educational value of *Huck Finn* as it was currently taught.

The Principal responded immediately to my letter by pulling my son out of English class and sending him to the library where he was instructed to work on something else. When the Principal called to tell me of his actions, I did not immediately object to his taking my son out of class because I was more concerned as to what the school's response was going to be to my request to have the book discontinued as required reading. Our phone conversation was very brief, however, and the Principal said very little beyond informing me that the forms needed to challenge class materials were being mailed to me.

In retrospect, the school's first action was awkward at best, perhaps symptomatic of the staff's inexperience in dealing with matters relating to race. Had officials been more willing to discuss the "incident," it certainly would have gone a long way towards reducing the racial tension and suspicion on both sides which, in turn, may have had an ameliorative effect on the final resolution of this matter. Since this was not the case, I had no alternative but to proceed to formally challenge the book's use. In effect, the battle-lines were drawn before there was ample opportunity to discuss the nature of the conflict or even establish a climate for discussion.

Fortunately, Christmas vacation intervened, providing time to step back from the situation, to reflect and to do some research in this area. I had, however, no further contact with the Principal, the teacher or any of the school district officials until March of 1982, when the paperwork detailing objections to the book was formally submitted to the district. (The "Citizen's Request for Reconsideration of a Book" was a one-page questionnaire asking for specific examples from the book for each stated objection. I gave seven objections and the completed form was some five pages long. I am grateful that I had the expert assistance of Dr. Jane Madsen, a professor of education at Penn State, whose specialty is identifying racism and sexism in children's literature.)

In April, my husband and I participated in two rather heated meetings involving the Supervisor of Secondary Education and the District English Coordinator. During these discussions, while apologies were offered for the teacher's blunder (the words "stupidity" and "insensitivity" were used) and for the embarrassment and pain it caused our son, neither the Supervisor nor the English Coordinator could understand that the teacher's remarks were, in and of themselves, racist and discriminatory in nature.

Fighting Between Whites and Blacks

As a district, we went through the "we shouldn't censor *Huck* but educate kids about its racism" stage about five years ago....

Regarding the effects of racist literature on students' attitudes and behavior, we found that exposure to Twain's constant use of the term "nigger" prompted white students' use of it freely and openly in school, resulting in an increase of angry interchanges and fights between white and Black students.

Ruth A. Gudinas, *Bulletin*, vol. 15, nos. 7/8, 1984.

In fact, the English Coordinator, who spent a good deal of time explaining the desired educational objectives involved in teaching the book, preferred that we avoid any discussion regarding the teacher's competence. We were asked to focus our concerns *solely* on the book. That focus led to an agreement between the School District and ourselves to put our "Request for Reconsideration" on hold while a Study Group was formed to identify the positive and negative effects of reading *Huck Finn* at the ninth-grade level. I consented to be part of the Study Group because the Supervisor of Secondary Education seemed to be very empathetic about our concerns, and both my husband and I had every hope that the issue would be resolved to our satisfaction. (The English Coordinator, however, continued to defend the book's literary and educational value.)

In the initial meetings of this Study Group, I was adamant in expressing my feeling that any book that permits an otherwise competent teacher to openly discriminate in class should not be required reading. My inclination was still to find fault with the book rather than the teacher; this may have been a strategic and critical error on my part.

During the next 18 months, the Study Group met some 16 times. Eventually—after much struggle—two recommendations were made. They were, very briefly:

(1) To use a book other than *Huck Finn* as required reading for ninth-grade classes but make it available for use in courses for grades eleven and twelve; and

(2) To undertake a comprehensive study of the schools' sensitivity to and treatment of minority groups in the curricula for grades K-12. (A Task Force on Understanding Others was set up to meet this recommendation.)

Racism Not Addressed

Reasonable as these recommendations sound, they unfortunately failed to address the real underlying issue of institutional racism. This often happens when educators over-intellectualize problems rooted in racial prejudice. Whites, in particular, find it very hard to identify, accept and understand their own racism and the way in which institutions, including the educational system, contribute to and perpetuate this racism.

At any rate, pressure from the School District to bring closure to this whole matter resulted in conclusions being drawn from the study that were not totally sound and which warranted further statistical analysis. Even worse, the study seemed to suggest (in the face of evidence to the contrary) that reading *Huck Finn* did not encourage stereotypic thinking in ninth graders. This study, which, to my dismay, bears my name as group member, has been distributed in a number of arenas, the most significant being the 1983 National Council of Teachers of English Convention.

Significantly, the printed study's recommendation that the book be held for the last two grades of high school was ignored. The School Board stated that it was not the Board's prerogative to decide the grade placement of the book, and that decision was referred to an English Advisory Committee made up of the English Coordinator and classroom teachers. At a School Board meeting in October, 1983, the final decision was to retain *Huck Finn* in the ninth grade.

The District did give the assurance that, prior to teaching the novel this year, in order to allow parents and youngsters to decide whether they wanted to read the book or not, letters would be sent to all parents informing them that the book had recently come under scrutiny because of the controversy surrounding its negative racial stereotyping of Blacks and its abundant use of racial slurs.

The School District never sent such a letter; it later decided to offer *Huck Finn* as one of three titles ninth graders could select for English class. (The other two books were also about adolescence: *Great Expectations* and *A Separate Peace*.)...

Two Supportive Events

Two separate but related events occurred...to change this entire picture for me. The first of these was reading the article, *"Huckleberry Finn and the Traditions of Blackface Minstrelsy"* in the CIBC [Council on Interracial Books for Children] *Bulletin*. This comprehensive piece, which brought some new historical and scholarly insights to understanding the negative characterization of Jim, underpinned academically many of the concerns that had been expressed nationwide about the book at a more emotional level.

The second thing that happened was that I was asked to participate in a panel on the teaching of *Huck Finn* in the public schools, at the Conference on American Comedy: A Celebration of 100 Years of *Huckleberry Finn*, hosted by Penn State in April. The panel presentation resulted in a very extensive and positive dialogue. And, while there was by no means a consensus, there was substantive agreement that indeed there are problems in teaching the novel; that it should be held for use in college or, at the earliest, in the upper grades of high school; and that new teaching strategies *must* be developed to properly teach the novel.

I came out of this conference buoyed and more committed than ever to the belief that no youngsters should be required to read literature which demeans, dehumanizes and caricatures their racial or ethnic heritage. Several years ago, *The Merchant of Venice* was dropped from a State College required reading list for this very reason. Why is *Huck Finn* immune from similar scrutiny?

Currently, the Pennsylvania NAACP Education Committee is fully supportive of my complaint, but the bureaucratic wheels of the Human Relations Commission are moving at a much slower pace. With or without their support, I intend to continue to fight this issue....

Bringing new insights, visions and perspectives to the teaching of *Huck Finn* is no easy matter. The book is cherished; its worth is passed down from professor to graduate student, from teacher to teacher, from teacher to student. But whatever the book's merits, there is a cost to pay in reading it, and unfortunately that cost is borne in large part by young Black students who may experience a complex range and mix of feelings from indifference to anger, from insult to humiliation. (There is also a cost to white students, whose out-dated notions of white superiority are reinforced.) No one has yet proven that the price we pay is reflected in positive educational gains for any student.

"Rather than ban books, let's create incentives to attract capable people to teaching."

'Huckleberry Finn' Is Not a Racist Novel

Shelley Fisher Fishkin

Shelley Fisher Fishkin, Ph.D., teaches American studies at the University of Texas at Austin. She is the author of *From Fact to Fiction: Journalism and Imaginative Writing in America*. In the following viewpoint, she describes *Huckleberry Finn* as "one of the greatest antiracist works of fiction ever written." The fault of racism lies not in the book, she claims, but in the manner in which the book is taught.

As you read, consider the following questions:

1. What reasons does the author give for using fiction along with history for studies in racism?
2. According to the author, what was the purpose of irony in Twain's works?
3. How does the experience of the author's son in the previous viewpoint compare with the experience of the black student mentioned in this viewpoint?

Shelley Fisher Fishkin, " 'Huck Finn' Is Hard to Read, Hard to Teach—But Worth It," *Minneapolis Star and Tribune*, June 9, 1985. Reprinted with the author's permission.

Mark Twain hated anniversaries. Maybe he knew something. This triple anniversary year [1985]—150 years after his birth, 75 years after his death, 100 years after the publication in this country of "Adventures of Huckleberry Finn"—has brought both plaudits and punches.

There's an impressive exhibit in Washington, sponsored by National Geographic and the Mark Twain Memorial, that will tour the country. An anniversary volume of essays has been published. Centennial conferences and lectures have been held, and a musical based on Twain's work is playing on Broadway.

Meanwhile, a spate of vituperative attacks on "Huckleberry Finn" as "racist trash" that "ought to be burned" has resumed.

A Great Antiracist Work

One of the greatest antiracist works of fiction ever written, "Huckleberry Finn" has been charged in the last 30 years with being "racist" in Illinois, New York, Iowa, Pennsylvania, Texas, Virginia and Canada, where efforts have been mounted to ban the book from the classroom.

In Hartford, several teachers continue to boycott the tours of Twain's home because they don't want their students exposed to a "racist" writer, and protesters tried to stop a Chicago stage production of "Huckleberry Finn" this winter.

Even an imagination as drenched with irony as Twain's would have had a hard time imagining the kind of trouble that has continued to embroil this book 100 years after it first appeared.

Twain's Letter

Last March [1985] some new ammunition for Twain's defenders surfaced from Twain himself: a letter written in Hartford the year "Huckleberry Finn" was published, pledging his support for one of the first black law students at Yale. That Twain had done something of this kind was of no news to Twain scholars (although the language of the letter—the direct, succinct condemnation of racism—was), but it was news to those who had been calling Twain a racist.

The media's response when I was fortunate enough to turn up the now-famous "McGuinn letter" might best be described as jubilant. Twain fans (the nation's newsrooms are filled with them) had something new to point to in Twain's defense.

But the critics didn't let up. Some continued to take a hard line: It's fine that Twain helped a black student here or there, but it's still a "racist" book (they cited the number of times the word "nigger" is used).

Others took a softer line: All right, it's not a racist book, but it's too hard to get that point across to high school students. They all agreed on one point: The book belongs out of the classroom.

No one ever said "Huckleberry Finn" is easy to teach. The book begins with the statement, "NOTICE: Persons attempting to find a motive in this narrative will be prosecuted; persons attempting to find a moral in it will be banished; persons attempting to find a plot in it will be shot. BY ORDER OF THE AUTHOR."

Twain meant to issue a warning of sorts: This book is going to be tough going, and if you're up for an easy read, turn back.

Twain first developed the distinctive brand of irony that characterizes "Huckleberry Finn" when, as a young reporter in San Francisco in the 1860s, he found that more straightforward exposes of racism would be censored. But irony is hard to understand and hard to teach.

"Why bother?" say those who want the book out of high schools. If it's important for students to understand slavery, these critics say, let them read history.

Fiction vs. History

I have no case to make against history. I'm all for it. But I'm deeply troubled by the notion that great works of fiction like "Huckleberry Finn" could be taken out of the classroom and replaced by history. Fiction must remain a central part of any education, especially fiction as difficult as "Huckleberry Finn."

Huck Finn Is No Racist

Anyone who labels *Huckleberry Finn* "racist trash" does not recognize that the principal purpose of the novel was to describe an ignorant 14-year-old boy's awakening to the injustices of slavery....In his flight with Jim, Huck denies everything—his people, his country, his God...this boy believes that there are laws greater than men's laws. Like Martin Luther King, Jr., Huck concludes that if a law be unjust, one has the right to break it. If Huck is a racist, then God help the country.

Michael Patrick Hearn, *School Library Journal*, February 1985.

The reader may be able to dismiss the people in history books as belonging to a distant past, to a different world from his own. Fiction writers, on the other hand, establish an emotional intimacy between their readers and their fictional creations; the reader is forced, in the greatest works of fiction, to care deeply about what happens to the characters.

Rather than being "racist trash" as its critics claim, "Huckleberry Finn" is an intensely moral book. It teaches the importance of constantly guarding against violations of people's self-respect and human dignity. It points up the danger of going along with institutional violence and hypocrisy.

It forces us to confront that part of ourselves that is still vulnerable to racism. It urges us to weigh the law of our country against the law of our conscience. It challenges us to exercise moral courage in the face of whatever obstacles we find in our path.

A Challenge to Teach

These are not easy lessons, and "Huckleberry Finn" is a challenge to teach. But if our teachers are not up to the challenge, the fault is ours, not Twain's. Rather than ban books, let's create incentives to attract capable people to teaching.

The stakes couldn't be higher: a generation steeped in know-nothingism, ignorance and fear, or one capable of grappling with the moral, emotional and intellectual challenges that life offers.

It may be cheaper to ban books than to fund education. But that doesn't mean we can afford it.

Recently I received a call from a great-great-niece of the black law student Twain had helped in 1885. She was delighted to read about the distinguished career of her great-great-uncle and was pleased that the letter's discovery had helped Twain out at a time when he needed it.

She told me that her son's teacher had asked her earlier this year how she'd feel if his 10th-grade class, in which there were only a handful of black students, read "Huckleberry Finn." She said that if it were taught with any sensitivity at all it would be fine. She'd always liked Twain. Her husband had, too.

Pride of Character

The first few discussions were hard on her son, she said. He couldn't get used to hearing the word "nigger" so often. But then his discomfort yielded to something else: pride. Pride in the strength of character that made Jim one of the most memorable and admirable figures in American literature, and pride in the strength that enabled his people to survive the brutality of slavery.

He told his mother that the book opened the eyes of his white classmates. It helped them understand, for the first time, some of what it felt like to be black. It helped them confront their own racism and the racism that persists in our society.

Reading that book, she said, was one of her son's most important experiences in high school.

I can date my love affair with literature and criticism—and with the frustrating and joyful project of grappling with the complexities of a work of art—to my own first encounter with "Huckleberry Finn" in high school. Now, nearly 20 years later, I find myself at the barricades defending the right of other high school students to read the book. I'm glad to be there.

Yes, it's hard to teach. Yes, it's hard to read. But yes, it's worth the trouble.

"The reality...is to know that while life is better than 20 years ago, [blacks] still are treated, seen and identified on the basis of [their] color."

White Racism Obstructs Black Progress

Juan Williams

In the following viewpoint, Juan Williams states that many people quote statistics demonstrating that blacks are much better off today than they were twenty years ago. However, writes Mr. Williams, the improvements for blacks are actually minimal. The vast majority are still far behind whites in earning power, education, status, and opportunity. The reason for this, he claims, is that, contrary to the views of complacent whites, racism is still prevalent.

As you read, consider the following questions:

1. Mr. Williams lists statistics which show the improvements in black life in the US over the past twenty years. Why does he believe these improvements are less significant than many people say they are?
2. Mr. Williams writes that "the worst form of the alienation blacks experience today comes from their inability to communicate with whites who don't see or hear the reality that blacks live." What does he mean by this statement?

Juan Williams, "So You Think Blacks Are Better Off Today Than 20 Years Ago?" *The Washington Post*, April 15, 1985. © The Washington Post. Reprinted with permission.

In its 1968 report on race in America, the Kerner Commission, sounding a doomsday voice above the sirens of race riots and assassinations, forecast that the United States was becoming two countries—one white and one black.

It was wrong. Today blacks and whites can be seen mixing at work, in the most expensive shopping malls, playing sports, running for office. Where the races separate is in the yawning gulf growing ever larger between black and white perceptions of politics and life.

Go ask whites what they think of Louis Farrakhan, leader of the Nation of Islam. Now go across town and ask blacks.

Go ask whites what they think of Jesse Jackson and Ronald Reagan. Then go to black political meetings and ask the same question. While there, ask blacks about the booming economy that whites celebrate. Ask blacks if life in America is better for them today than it was 20 years ago; then go ask whites.

From the two tribes come answers so different that it is now apparent that while they do live together, black and white Americans are divorced.

Whites, like Ronald Reagan, want to talk about how different 1985 is from 1965. They're right. [Black stars] Eddie Murphy and Bill Cosby as the kings of comedy is different. Black mayors in Chicago, Los Angeles, Philadelphia and Washington is different. The sight of black faces among the police, judges, TV news people and in corporate America is different. A black running for president is different.

On that basis the president asks why black leaders don't celebrate the good progress of the past 20 years. And whites, generally, ask: Why are blacks so alienated?

Trapped in No Man's Land

The answer: To be a black American in 1985 is to be trapped in a no man's land. The trap is to listen to whites happily tell you that the battle against racism has been won, the world is colorblind, you can compete and make it on your own.

The reality, to black eyes, however, is to know that while life is better than 20 years ago, you still are treated, seen and identified on the basis of your color. And while black incomes are up in absolute terms, and blatant discrimination is down, to be black is to feel the power of U.S. Census Bureau statistics showing that in 1959 blacks were three times as likely as whites to be poor, and in 1983, the last year for which comparable figures are available, they were still three times as likely as whites to be poor.

Whites take it as gospel, almost without exception, that blacks have a better life today than they did 20 years ago. Yet while black family income has risen along with that of other Americans, the median income of black families today is about $8,000 less than that of whites. That's the same gap, in constant dollars, that existed in

181

1966.

Similarly, in 1965 white male unemployment was 3.6 percent versus 7.4 percent for black men. Today it is 6.6 percent for white men and 13.7 for black men.

Life is better for blacks; their standard of living as a group has improved, and educated blacks are approaching parity in income with whites. The black middle class has increased in size and income. While 4.8 percent of the people in college were black in 1965, 10.2 percent were in 1984.

Advances Did Not End Racism

The battles that put an end to segregation in public restaurants, other public places and on public transportation were important advances. But they did not finish off racism.

The breakthroughs in hiring and even promotion in basic industry were very important. But they also did not end racism.

The advances in housing, education, medical care and culture are all very important. But they also have not eliminated racism.

Many of the affirmative action programs have corrected some of the inequalities, have compensated for some of the effects of long-term practices of discrimination. But they have not by any means done away with all inequalities.

There have been welcome changes in the thought patterns of millions. But the racist poison, the thought patterns that are influenced by racism and chauvinism, have not been eradicated.

Gus Hall, *Daily World*, February 28, 1985.

So, some say, isn't it really true that blacks who are not properly educated, who have children as teen-agers, who get involved in crime and drugs, are dragging down blacks as a group more than any white racist?

Victimized by Racism

The answer is yes. But how is it possible to identify that underclass as anything but a group highly victimized by the racism that remains in the country? Certainly some of their problems are of their own making. Upright young people, who work hard in cold tenements, go to school and have jobs afterward, might make it out. But that is not to say that their educationally deprived, culturally poor parents and grandparents, and their jobless parents and friends, don't make for a sick environment that hampers their success.

In addition, much of the progress of the past 20 years has halted. The number of blacks in college doubled from 1965 to 1975, but it has remained about the same ever since, even though the percentage of blacks completing high school has gone up. The number of blacks making more than $25,000 in constant dollars, which doubled from 1965 to 1975, dropped between 1975 to 1985. For black men the drop was from 11.7 percent to 10.8 percent; for black women it was from 2.5 percent to 2.3 percent.

But to whites the question persists: Aren't blacks better off today than they were 20 years ago? The naiveté of the question baffles, and alienates, blacks. In a TV interview during the 20th anniversary of the Montgomery-to-Selma march, Jesse Jackson was prodded by a local reporter to comment on the rise in elected officials in the state and nation in the past 20 years. In 1970 there were 1,469 elected black officials, and in 1984 there were 5,700.

Jackson replied that there is a huge gulf between "participation and parity." He said blacks constitute about 1 percent of all elected officials although they are more than 10 percent of the population. The white TV reporter looked shocked at the reply.

Half a Loaf

Listen closely, white America, to what Jackson said. There is more political power for blacks in the form of more elected officials; but there is no equality. And blacks are angry that whites would have them celebrate having gained half a loaf, while whites still have the whole loaf.

An example: Many in the black middle class today feel that being smart and working hard doesn't guarantee success. They fear that all their efforts will be for nothing if whites don't feel the need to hire and promote a token black face.

Many blacks feel that their hard work will probably go unnoticed or they will run into white competitors who might not be as good but who are in the right, white, circles; they are more comfortable for the boss to deal with. As black mothers still tell their children: "You've got to be twice as good to go half as far as a white."

But that's not the way whites see it. An article by Charles Murray, a white conservative thinker, called "Affirmative Racism—How Preferential Treatment Works Against Blacks," in the Dec. 31 [1984] issue of *The New Republic*, argued that racism is being renewed among whites because whites find work done by blacks to be second-rate. Murray writes that whites accept the shoddy work and keep blacks in the best of jobs, in the best schools, to fulfill the need for black faces. That not only leaves whites resentful but leaves blacks, Murray continues, with the anxiety of feeling they've been hired only because they are black.

From a white perspective, Murray may be right, although many whites have castigated him. But surely from a black perspective he has created a fantastic tower of myths.

Companies do sometimes hire unqualified blacks and keep them for the sake of having blacks in house. But are blacks to believe that if not for them the white world would be a total meritocracy? The

"Peter Principle" promotion of people to their level of incompetence is hardly a black invention.

Here's the news from black America: Blacks in America are different because of race. They are victims of racism yesterday and today. It's a different brand of racism today, and I offer you...stories of racism, 1985-style; the bitter reality of black life in a land where blacks are equal in the eyes of the law, but where life is more than the law.

Major Area of Alienation

The major public area of alienation for blacks is politics.

Even Republicans will happily tell reporters that [Presidential candidate] Jesse Jackson's treatment by white Democrats has been a "disgrace."...

To a majority of blacks who see in Jackson a stirring leader amid lesser lights in the Democratic Party, it is frustrating to see so many whites simply acknowledge that they can't vote for a black man and find so many reasons to justify it. Whites can argue that they prefer [Gary] Hart's ideas, or [Walter] Mondale's policies. But to blacks in the political grandstand, Jackson's proposals and ideas seem not so much rejected as not considered. And the reason is Jackson is not seen as a serious candidate because he is black. His leadership ability counts for nothing with white Democrats who prefer to set him aside as the black leader.

Keeping Blacks Down

Black people in America, despite enormously significant political gains in the 1960s and 1970s, do not yet possess real political power because we as a people are far removed from economic empowerment in this nation.

Economic power is political power and political power is economic power; and there are those in America who do not want Black citizens to have either. If we can prevail in this present adverse economic climate—and we shall prevail—we will be well on the way towards the achievement of economic parity.

Parren J. Mitchell, *engage/social action*, November 1980.

To some white eyes, blacks seem emotionally, if not irrationally, attached to Jackson and his demagogic style of politicking. White critics rightly note that Jackson is criticized by his peers—black politicians—for having an inflated ego, for being a maverick and for not following through on all the plans in his foot-stomping speeches. They note the smell of scandal that lingers around Jackson, with government investigations of his organization, PUSH, for improper use of money. They also point to Jackson's ties to anti-American leaders like [Fidel] Castro and [Yasser] Arafat.

Now for the black perspective: Why don't whites apply the same standard to, let's say, Ronald Reagan. Didn't a flag-and-Bible-waving Reagan write a letter in 1960 attacking John Kennedy as a closet communist for ideas that boiled down to putting a new face on "old Karl Marx....Hitler called his [version of Kennedy's ideas] state socialism"? Don't large numbers of white voters go pep-rally crazy over Reagan's demagogic support of school prayer, getting tough on criminals and stopping abortion? For that matter, questions were raised about Mondale's use of labor's political action committee money during the primary campaign, and Hart was noticed changing his name and age.

So, why is Jackson dismissed by whites as a serious political voice for sins that are blips on the screen for his white counterparts?...

In every case there is a hint that black politicians who are less concerned with issues identified as black concerns will succeed in the long run while the Jacksons of the political world who focus on their black constituency will fail.

Corporate Racism

This tale comes from a 30-year-old Ivy League graduate who played high school basketball with me, an eight-year management-level employee in a Philadelphia bank, educated and with a very middle-class salary.

To drink a beer with him and talk about his professional life is to listen to an alienated man who feels victimized by being black.

After his last promotion he went to work on a group project where he was the only black employee out of nearly 20. He saw challenging assignments given to other young executives and, from his perspective, felt that the boss didn't think the only black on his staff was up to the work. But, said my pal, a Phi Beta Kappa, "I was going to show him I could do it."

Yet, digging in to establish himself, he thought he found his good work taken without comment, but any slip-up an occasion for every boss to be shown his failings.

As my friend tells it, his commitment still didn't slack off. He would work until everyone had left the office to prove his commitment. He bought new suits; and, laughing, remembers buying new deodorants and mouth washes, buying a new car, even, and offering his colleagues rides home.

It didn't help. He tried to recruit a mentor for himself but ran into slow going. "I was never invited to the dinner parties with the vice presidents unless the [city] politicians were there, and that was to have a black face in the group," he said.

The situation caused my friend an identity crisis: He became anxious when another black was brought onto the management staff. Having lost the sense that his hard work and smarts could set him apart, he worried that even his lone status among whites—as the only black—was being taken away.

He complained; management's eyes glazed over. They wanted to deal with success, not racial problems, they said. Pretty soon he began hearing that the higher-ranking managers were questioning his ability; one rumor was that maybe he was promoted only because he was black; for sure he was moved up too quickly. Worst of all, he was not sure his feelings were not due to his own paranoia. He worried that he might not be up to the job.

Black Alienation

Here then is an alienated, angry young black face that whites can see in the corporate world. Why are you alienated? they ask. If you are going to be moody and angry, why don't you leave?

Whites, like the Reagan administration, are dead set on a color-blind society that would neglect not only the history of black-white relations in America, but neglects the reality of current life for blacks in America. There is an advantage to being white. There is a disadvantage to being black. That is why, if whites legitimately want an integrated society, a welcome hand, in the form of goals for getting blacks into companies, as well as a helping hand to watch their career, should be extended.

Short of that, it can lead to a conclusion that blacks should be separate from whites. Black thinkers as diverse as Clarence Pendleton, conservative chairman of the U.S. Civil Rights Commission; James Meredith, the civil rights activist who integrated the University of Mississippi 23 years ago, and Louis Farrakhan, the Nation of Islam leader, agree that desegregation has not helped black America.

Racism Thrives

Since racism is a white problem, whites must first confront it in themselves. But it is precisely because they haven't done this that racism still thrives in America.

George M. Daniels, *engage/social action*, October 1981.

"Integration hurt black neighborhoods, hurt black businesses, destroyed black families," Pendleton told me. "You make your choice in this country. You can live black, buy black, work black ...or you can live like you are white, drive a BMW...until discrimination hits you. And if you're going to get hit by discrimination, the only thing you can do is go back and live black."

Maybe the worst form of the alienation blacks experience today comes from their inability to communicate with whites who don't see or hear the reality that blacks live.

I was sitting in a restaurant with James Meredith when he repeated to the diners that he felt integration had become a "sham."

186

The only real difference between America 20 years ago and America today is that blacks can eat in restaurants, sleep in hotels, get jobs in the big corporations, he said. They still don't have equality of power. A white at the table, looking at the black college admissions staff worker from a white school and at a black journalist representing my paper, said Meredith must be fooling. Meredith's face tightened. He said nothing.

Later, in private, he said to me that whites are happy with the idea that civil rights is history; it means they don't have to face what remains of racism. "They can politely stay away from blacks as if that is the right thing to do," he said. "I'd rather be lynched than ignored."

Different Black and White Visions

I don't know that I'd prefer to die, but being unable to communicate with whites on any key issue involving race is intolerable. And that emerges most explosively in the differing visions blacks and whites have of current events.

Take Louis Farrakhan. Last year he made widely reported comments offensive to Jews such as calling Hitler a "wickedly great" man. The Jewish and white outrage could not be contained. But what really baffled whites was that there was no parallel concern in the black community. Why is Farrakhan, even now, regarded seriously by blacks, whites ask?

For many blacks I know, at least, their outrage was absent because what they heard was Farrakhan saying that Hitler was an historic figure who did evil. That sounded right to them.

I find this walled-off reality between blacks and whites, in business, in politics, in current events, the stunning reality of life 20 years after the great civil rights movement that was to bring black and white together. That legacy is one my black friends nod at, with sad knowing, and my white friends nod off at, asking what do blacks have to complain about, they're on TV....

Whites don't seem to care that blacks are saying America today is just as alienating and infuriating to them as it was 20 years ago. They don't want to hear it.

"What started out as black pride eventually turned into black racism."

Black Racism Obstructs Black Progress

Ian Gilbert and William Hough

Ian Gilbert is a lawyer and member of the editorial staff of *The Washington Times*. William Hough is a free-lance writer and retired army staff sergeant. Both writers, the former white, the latter black, believe that blacks in the US have not advanced as much as they might have. The reason, they argue in the following viewpoint, is not the oft-blamed white racism. Instead, the cause is the racism of blacks themselves.

As you read, consider the following questions:

1. What evidence does each writer give of the existence of black racism?
2. In what sense, according to Mr. Hough, is black racism "destroying [blacks] as a race"?
3. What does Mr. Hough believe blacks must do to "catch up" with whites?

Ian Gilbert, "Playing Switcheroo with Racial Bias," *The Washington Times*, February 28, 1985. Reprinted with the author's permission. William Hough, "On Being Black in America," *The Washington Times*, August 14, 1984. Reprinted with permission.

I

Something very wrong is happening in American race relations; there's an ugly resurgence of skin-color prejudice, and it's coming from a quarter that shocks this self-styled white liberal. Consider these excerpts from a recent newspaper article:

"...many of the parents...want to inculcate in their children a deep respect for their own white identity and for white people." A ninth-grade girl's "mother...helped her daughter make up the [school dance] guest list to ensure that white boys...were invited." Said the mother, "I know she knows she is white. I'm always going to keep her mindful that she is white, and I want her to help [her school] understand what whiteness is all about."

Then there is the mother, quoted by another journalist, who heard a new song on her daughter's stereo and asked, "Who is it? Sounds like somebody black." Depressed at her daughter's answer, the mother tells us, "As far as I am concerned we are dealing with the continued existence of white people."

Conjures up decades-old images of white bigots, doesn't it, the folks who screamed obscenities at busloads of black kids on their way to their newly integrated schools. Or we see in our mind's eye a Southern governor of long ago, preaching white supremacy and the horrors of miscegenation. Didn't this kind of talk disappear from respectable discourse 20 years ago?

Yes, it did. My quotes are fraudulent; in the original articles, "black" appeared where I used "white," and "white" was used where I've substituted "black." Am I the only one who finds this offensive?

Black "Identity"?

This kind of black racism, masquerading as "black identity" or "black culture," has been showing up with increasing frequency in recent years; no matter what the euphemism—compare "white pride"—it's still racism.

The first excrescence of this viciousness was the "black English" tempest of a few years back, the preposterous notion that business, government, and society should accord respect to a primitive, unsophisticated language of severely limited vocabulary, a grammar heavily biased toward the present tense, punctuation marks unprintable in a family newspaper, and all-but-incomprehensible diction.

If there's any argument at all for the "black is beautiful" syndrome, it's that black kids subjected to direct white racist assaults on their self-esteem should have an antidote. That there are still towns and neighborhoods where such assaults occur, there can be no doubt.

But the mothers I quoted at the beginning of this essay are bemoaning the fates of their daughters in fancy private schools in

Washington, D.C. The teen listening to her stereo never had anyone call her "nigger" until she was 16—by which age several black youths had already called me names or tried to push me off the sidewalk for no apparent reason other than my skin color.

The last time a student of "black pride" called me a "honky" in public is still fresh in my mind, and it's happened to me several times in recent years. Is that what "black identity" is all about, justifying hatred and bigotry, offering an easy explanation for the fact that not everyone—black, white, red, or yellow—can be a bank president?

Blaming Others

I have observed in many black clients a tendency to inappropriately blame society to evade personal responsibility for their actions....

Black leaders must realize that if every white person vanished from the face of the earth, there still would be far too much Black-on-Black crime; alcoholism; drug abuse; domestic violence; poor work habits; divorce; etc.

Peter Bell, *Lincoln Review*, Summer 1984.

All through the civil rights upheavals of the '50s and '60s, all but the most diehard bigots were offended, even angered, by white supremacists' public pronouncements about racial "differences," black "inferiority," biological arguments for segregation—in short, anything suggesting that skin color is more than skin deep. Decent people ostracized anyone expressing such ideas.

Patronizing Black Racism

Yet now, when blacks openly and without apparent embarrassment rehash in perhaps politer terms the same old skin-color prejudices, no one says anything. Why? I suspect that some conservatives, still uncomfortable with the obsolete association of "conservative" with "Southern"—the anti-civil rights filibusterers of 20 to 30 years ago—are afraid to criticize black racism because they think they'll be called racists themselves.

Among my liberal friends are some who won't criticize blacks—or any other politically fashionable minority, for that matter—for ideological reasons—a racial bias, perhaps, against non-blacks. Others have privately expressed their agreement with my anger at black racism, but, in what seems to me to be the worst sort of patronizing tone, shrug their shoulders as if to ask, "What can you expect?"

You can expect—indeed, must expect—those who have fought hardest for and most benefited from the end of official racism to give as good as they've gotten. The civil rights struggle was too hard-fought by too many Americans, to have its success mocked by continuing racism from persons of any hue.

II

No race has a monopoly on prejudice and racism. This reality seems to escape today's predominant black thought pattern. Yet the overall lot of our people would surely improve if we black Americans weren't so preoccupied with the question of race; we literally see everything in the terms of black and white. There are very good reasons why blacks should be somewhat skeptical when dealing with some whites, but to prejudge every person because he or she is white is just plain ludicrous. We have been accusing whites of this very same offense for years. Now there is no other ethnic group in America that seems more prejudiced than us blacks. And it is virtually destroying us as a race. The black media, the black leaders, and our parents must share in the blame for this.

Black Pride

Back in the 1960s the civil rights movement brought with it assertiveness, black power, and black pride. Black pride became perhaps, the greatest symbol of the entire movement. It took many forms—colorful dashikis, bush hair styles, to name a few. Carrying a copy of *Soul on Ice*, for example, earned super recognition. For some, black pride also meant to call white people honkies, to give the black power salute, and even saying anything that came into one's mind, anytime, any place, no matter how offensive.

For others, black pride meant that we would be accepted into almost any college regardless of our qualifications or our academic background. All we had to do was to prove that we had stumbled through some high school. We were practically assured of graduating by just attending the required amount of time. We also know that we would not flunk out no matter how poorly we performed because we would yell racist to the top of our lungs. We knew that no one wanted to be labeled a racist. So why not take advantage of these well-meaning people? After all, we seemed to have the approval of our black leaders and black media, but most of all the approval of our parents. Not one of these groups or individuals had taken the time to explain that black pride wasn't worth a damn without responsibility. For instance, no one told us that a responsible person had to get the best education possible and to respect others as well as ourselves; that courtesy is reciprocal and that discipline must be maintained in all our endeavors and must be reflected throughout our lives.

Black Racism

Since these institutions failed to get this simple message across, what we have today is over-crowded jails (probably 85 percent black), a community of hate-filled functional illiterates who will be

191

wards of the city, county, state, or federal government probably all of their lives. Why?...because what started out as black pride eventually turned into black racism. How can we see racism and prejudice in other races but fail to recognize it among ourselves?

We are constantly bombarded with negativism by our black press. For instance, we are fed depressing information about this wicked one-sided society that we live in and that our chance of making it is almost nil. And if we just happen to make it, we will have to be twice as good as a white person doing the same job. We hear this same kind of negativism from family, friends, and neighbors. No wonder so many young blacks are tuned out and turned off. We end up with an embittered and confused individual. No employer is going to hire a person with an attitudinal problem. No one wants a person around who is unable to cope with people of different races. Yet, we wonder why foreign blacks who come to these shores do well. We are quick to criticize them and call them Uncle Toms because they work so cheaply. Yet within five years these foreign blacks often are well on their way to realizing their dreams.

Black Racism Harms

During a recent national speaking tour of Minister Louis Farrakhan, over 100,000 people turned out to hear him—30,000 at Madison Square Garden in New York....

According to Farrakhan, the main enemy of Afro-Americans is...the Jewish people in particular and white people in general. The Jews, he says, "through their stranglehold over the government" are responsible for the conditions of Afro-Americans. They are today's slavemaster and he is "tired of this slavemaster and slave relationship."...

It would be a dangerous mistake to deny or downplay [Louis] Farrakhan's anti-Semitism. He seeks to turn the longings of Afro-Americans for equality against the Jewish people, thereby sabotaging the struggle for equality and besmirching the outstanding contributions which Afro-Americans have made to the history of our country....

Farrakhan does not instill national pride among Afro-American youth. He betrays it.

Robert Lindsay, *Political Affairs*, December 1985.

We black Americans must understand that there is no short cut to success. We, like everyone else, must take the regular route. We can't wait for someone to invent the smart pill. Which means hitting the books when your friends are out singing, dancing, and playing sports. These extra-curricular activities are great if you can afford it. But from our position we can't do anything but catch up. We have been here for generations and still have problems with the only language we ever knew. That tells me that something is very wrong. In fact, if we ever intend to catch up, we have to cast aside our false pride, our racial prejudices, and get down to the [business of] becoming as educated as any citizens of our great land.

Rid Selves of Racial Animosity

No more excuses about the text-books and tests being culturally biased. No one has to prove anything to me. I know that we are capable of becoming just as educated as any other group. However, there are a lot of people out there who believe just the opposite. Not just racially motivated groups like the Klu Klux Klan or the American Nazi Party, but even some college professor has said that blacks are intellectually inferior to whites. It is up to us to prove these people wrong. It is also up to us to prove to the people with the money, jobs, and power that we can do the job. But first, we must rid ourselves of the racial animosity that is consuming our very soul. This will be even a harder task in the future, considering that the Rev. Jesse Jackson has allied with Louis Farrakhan— the most vicious anti-white individual that this nation has produced. When Mr. Farrakhan was the national spokesman for the Nation of Islam under the leadership of Elijah Muhammad, Mr. Farrakhan would speak each Sunday afternoon at 2 o'clock. When you heard this man speak it was just like listening to the Grand Wizard of the KKK or someone from Hitler's Nazi Party. Can you imagine what would happen if a white candidate from either party was seen associating with a leader from the KKK or the American Nazi Party?

We blacks must learn to think independently, and to vote our conscience. An educated person doesn't need an individual or a group of individuals to dictate how to vote. An educated person will make an independent decision, based on facts that are presented to him by an unbiased source. The easiest thing to pick up and the hardest thing to drop is prejudice.

Distinguishing Bias from Reason

When dealing with highly controversial subjects, many often will allow their feelings to dominate their powers of reason. Thus, one of the most important critical thinking skills is the ability to distinguish between statements based upon emotion and those based upon a rational consideration of the facts.

Most of the following statements are taken from the viewpoints in this chapter. Consider each statement carefully. *Mark R for any statement you believe is based on reason or a rational consideration of the facts. Mark B for any statement you believe is based on bias, prejudice, or emotion. Mark I for any statement you think is impossible to judge.*

If you are doing this activity as a member of a class or group, compare your answers with those of other class or group members. Be able to explain your answers. You may discover that others will come to different conclusions than you. Listening to the reasons others present for their answers may give you valuable insights in distinguishing between bias and reason.

If you are reading this book alone, ask others if they agree with your answers. You will find this interaction very valuable.

R = *a statement based upon reason*
B = *a statement based upon bias*
I = *a statement impossible to judge*

1. *Huckleberry Finn* is racist trash.

2. The study of fiction is the most essential part of any education.

3. *Huckleberry Finn* has been charged in the last 30 years with being racist in six states and Canada.

4. We are only creatures of politics.

5. *Huck Finn* is one of the greatest anti-racist works of fiction ever written.

6. For this argument we must make a distinction between what is public policy and what is private policy.

7. Affirmative action may be useful for an employer who recognizes a problem of racism, but it may not be useful for everyone.

8. Blacks would never get jobs without affirmative action.

9. The system of affirmative action is administered by one of the least competent bureaucracies in the federal government.

10. We should not expect affirmative action to solve all of America's minority unemployment problems.

11. Intellectuals value liberty only when it relates to themselves.

12. As the chart indicates, whites are the majority of beneficiaries in all but one of the nation's major welfare programs.

13. According to statistics, about three of the welfare recipients relegated to the "undeserving" category are black and Hispanic.

14. Most economists agree that three recessions and double-digit inflation have triggered economic reversals for blacks.

15. In our society, the interests of whites always prevail over the interests of blacks.

16. Statistics show that welfare rolls recently have been climbing faster in rural counties than in metropolitan areas.

17. Only a fool could think that discrimination is the primary cause of poverty among blacks.

Bibliography

The following list of books, periodicals, and pamphlets deals with the subject matter of this chapter.

Alan Ashkinaze   "A New Form of Racism," *New Guard*, Summer 1982.

Fred Barnes   "Farrakhan Frenzy," *The New Republic*, October 28, 1985.

Verne Becker   "The Counterfeit Christianity of the Ku Klux Klan, "*Christianity Today*, April 20, 1984.

Derek Bok   "Admitting Success," *The New Republic*, February 4, 1985.

Allan C. Carlson   "On 'Discrimination,' 'Prejudice,' and Other Ideological Disguises," *Persuasion at Work*, August 1984. Individual copies available for $1.00 from The Rockford Institute, 934 North Main Street, Rockford, IL 61103.

Ralph P. Davidson   "Keep Federal Affirmative Action Strong," *The New York Times*, November 25, 1985.

Robert F. Drinan   "Another Look at Affirmative Action," *America*, February 9, 1985.

Richard A. Hoehn   "Combating Racism: Touch and Tell," *The Christian Century*, March 3, 1982.

Charles Krauthammer   "A Defense of Quotas," *The New Republic*, September 16/23, 1985.

Julius Lester   "The Time Has Come," *The New Republic*, October 28, 1985.

Glenn C. Loury   "Beyond Civil Rights," *The New Republic*, October 7, 1985.

Harvey C. Mansfield Jr.   "The Underhandedness of Affirmative Action," *National Review*, May 4, 1984.

Charles Murray   "Affirmative Racism," *The New Republic*, December 31, 1984.

Philip Tajitsu Nash   "Asian Americans: 100 Years of Hate," *Guardian*, October 30, 1985.

Thomas Sowell   *Civil Rights: Rhetoric or Reality?* New York: William Morrow & Co., Inc., 1984.

Walter E. Williams   *The State Against Blacks*. New York: New Press/McGraw-Hill, 1984.

5 CHAPTER

The Nature of Racism

Introduction

In 1954, Gordon W. Allport published his classic study, *The Nature of Prejudice*. In it, Allport thoroughly analyzed the way in which prejudice is developed and reinforced in children and eventually becomes firmly established in adulthood. Allport's conclusions, supported today by an overwhelming consensus of biological and social scientists, stand as a definitive statement on the environmental origins of prejudice. It is for this reason that a lengthy excerpt from his book is presented as the opening viewpoint in the final chapter of this anthology on racism.

The remaining viewpoints in the chapter relate to Allport's environmental thesis. De Gobineau was a nineteenth-century French aristocrat who was painfully disenchanted with the egalitarianism which grew out of the French Revolution of 1789. Hitler was a chauvinistic German nationalist who believed that an international plot directed by racially inferior peoples was thwarting the superior Aryan's destined rise to world hegemony. Elijah Muhammad, the founder of the Black Muslim religion, was convinced that a conspiracy of evil emanating from America's white majority had enslaved and would continue to enslave America's blacks. Finally, the *UNESCO Statement on Race* is an authoritative declaration issued by a consortium of world scientists rejecting the archaic and dangerous notion of genetically inferior races.

Racism has been and continues to be one of the most divisive forces in human history. By its very nature, it can set nation against nation, friend against friend. Whether it is an inherent part of the human condition or simply a bizarre aberration nurtured in environments shrouded by hatred and prejudice, it is equally odious and destructive.

"A home that is suppressive, harsh, or critical —where the parent's word is law—is more likely to prepare the groundwork for group prejudice."

How Prejudice Is Learned

Gordon W. Allport

In 1954, Gordon W. Allport published his highly acclaimed book, *The Nature of Prejudice*. The origins of racist and prejudicial behavioral patterns in individuals and groups had long been debated among social and biological scientists. Allport's book was almost immediately heralded as being a classic statement on the environmental roots of these antisocial traits. A professor of psychology at Harvard University at the time, Professor Allport had devoted much of his academic career to studying the grounds and development of prejudice. His work is recognized still as one of the seminal and authoritative studies on the subject. In the following viewpoint, excerpted from *The Nature of Prejudice*, Professor Allport illustrates the subtle way in which prejudicial attitudes are developed in children.

As you read, consider the following questions:

1. What does the study by Harris, Gough and Martin reveal about the mothers of prejudiced children?
2. According to the author, what role does language play in the development of prejudice?

Gordon W. Allport, THE NATURE OF PREJUDICE, © 1954, Addison-Wesley, Reading, Massachusetts. Pgs. 297, 298, 299, 300, 301, 302, 304, 305, 307, 308, 309, 310 & 395 (excerpts). Reprinted with permission.

How is prejudice learned? We have opened our discussion of this pivotal problem by pointing out that the home influence has priority, and that the child has excellent reasons for adopting his ethnic attitudes ready-made from his parents....The first six years of life are important for the development of all social attitudes, though it is a mistake to regard early childhood as alone responsible for them. A bigoted personality may be well under way by the age of six, but by no means fully fashioned....

Child Training

One line of proof that a child's prejudice is related to the manner of his upbringing comes from a study of Harris, Gough, and Martin. These investigators first determined the extent to which 240 fourth, fifth, and sixth grade children expressed prejudiced attitudes toward minority groups. They then sent questionnaires to the mothers of these children, asking their views on certain practices in child training. Most of these were returned with the mothers' replies. The results are highly instructive. Mothers of prejudiced children, *far more often* than the mothers of unprejudiced children, held that

> Obedience is the most important thing a child can learn.
> A child should never be permitted to set his will against that
> of his parents.
> A child should never keep a secret from his parents.
> "I prefer a quiet child to one who is noisy."
> (In the case of temper tantrums) "Teach the child that two
> can play that game, by getting angry yourself."

In the case of sex-play (masturbation) the mother of the prejudiced child is much more likely to believe she should punish the child; the mother of the unprejudiced child is much more likely to ignore the practice.

All in all, the results indicate that pervasive family atmospheres do definitely slant the child. Specifically, a home that is suppressive, harsh, or critical—where the parents' word is law—is more likely to prepare the groundwork for group prejudice....

Power and Authority

What does such a style of child training do to a child? For one thing it puts him on guard. He has to watch his impulses carefully. Not only is he punished for them when they counter the parents' convenience and rules, as they frequently do, but he feels at such times that love is withdrawn from him. When love is withdrawn he is alone, exposed, desolate. Thus he comes to watch alertly for signs of parental approval or disapproval. It is they who have power, and they who give or withhold their conditional love. Their power and their will are the decisive agents in the child's life.

What is the result? First of all, the child learns that power and authority dominate human relationships—not trust and tolerance.

200

The stage is thus set for a hierarchical view of society. Equality does not really prevail. The effect goes even deeper. The child mistrusts his impulses: he must not have temper tantrums, he must not disobey, he must not play with his sex organs. He must fight such evil in himself. Through a simple act of projection the child comes to fear evil impulses in others. They have dark designs; their impulses threaten the child; they are not to be trusted....

In other words, prejudice was not *taught* by the parent but was *caught* by the child from an infected atmosphere....

Authoritarians and Prejudice

Authoritarians typically convey an idealized picture of their parents as near-perfect. Generalizing this unrealistic view to include other authorities, they come to view the world in good-bad, up-and-down power terms. They are outwardly submissive toward those they see as authorities with power over them, and aggressive toward those they see as beneath them in status. This hierarchical view of authority links directly with ethnic attitudes. High-status ethnic groups are respected, and authoritarians treat them with deference. But low-status ethnic groups are disparaged. Prejudice becomes for many authoritarians "a crutch upon which to limp through life." Lacking insight into their own inner feelings, they project their own unacceptable impulses onto outgroups whom they regard as beneath them.

Thomas F. Pettigrew, *Prejudice*, 1982.

Let us [turn] to the question whether there is an inborn source of prejudice....As soon as infants are able (perhaps at six months of age) to distinguish between familiar and unfamiliar persons, they sometimes show anxiety when strangers approach. They do so especially if the stranger moves abruptly or makes a "grab" for the child. They may show special fear if the stranger wears eyeglasses, or has skin of an unfamiliar color, or even if his expressive movements are different from what the child is accustomed to. This timidity usually continues through the preschool period—often beyond. Every visitor who has entered a home where there is a young child knows that it takes several minutes, perhaps several hours, for the child to "warm up" to him. But usually the initial fear gradually disappears.

We [conducted] an experiment where infants were placed alone in a strange room with toys. All of the children were at first alarmed and cried in distress. After a few repetitions they became entirely habituated to the room and played as if at home. But the biological utility of the initial fear reaction is obvious. Whatever is strange is a potential danger, and must be guarded against until one's experience assures one that no harm is lurking.

The almost universal anxiety of a child in the presence of strangers is no more striking than his rapid adaptability to their presence....

Dawn of Racial Awareness

The theory of "home atmosphere" is certainly more convincing than the theory of "instinctive roots." But neither theory tells us just when and how the child's ethnic ideas begin to crystallize. Granted that the child possesses relevant emotional equipment, and that the family supplies a constant undertone of acceptance or rejection, anxiety or security, we still need studies that will show how the child's earliest sense of group differences develops. An excellent setting for such a study is a biracial nursery school.

In investigations conducted in this setting, it appears that the earliest age at which children take any note of race is two and a half.

One white child of this age, sitting for the first time beside a Negro child, said, "Dirty face." It was an unemotional remark, prompted only by his observing a wholly dark-skinned visage—for the first time in his life.

The purely sensory observation that some skins are white, some colored, seems in many cases to be the first trace of racial awareness. Unless there is the quiver of fear of the strange along with this observation, we may say that race difference at first arouses a sense of curiosity and interest—nothing more. The child's world is full of fascinating distinctions. Facial color is simply one of them. Yet we note that even this first perception of racial difference may arouse associations with "clean" and "dirty."

The situation is more insistent by the age of three and a half or four. The sense of dirt still haunts the children. They have been thoroughly scrubbed at home to eradicate dirt. Why then does it exist so darkly on other children? One colored boy, confused concerning his membership, said to his mother, "Wash my face clean; some of the children don't wash well, expecially colored children."...

Initial Damage of Associated Ideas

Dr. Goodman's nursery school study shows one particularly revealing result. Negro children are, by and large, "racially aware" earlier than are white children. (Mary E. Goodman, *Race Awareness in Young Children.*) They tend to be confused, disturbed, and sometimes excited by the problem. Few of them seem to know that they are Negroes. (Even at the age of seven one little Negro girl said to a white playmate, "I'd hate to be colored, wouldn't you?")...

The initial damage of associated ideas seems inescapable in our culture. Dark skin suggests dirt—even to a four-year-old. To some it may suggest feces. Brown is not the aesthetic norm in our culture (in spite of the popularity of chocolate). But this initial disadvantage is by no means insuperable. Discriminations in the realm of color are not hard to learn: a scarlet rose is not rejected because it is the color of blood, nor a yellow tulip because it is the color of urine.

To sum up: four-year-olds are normally interested, curious, and appreciative of differences in racial groups. A slight sense of white superiority seems to be growing, largely because of the association of white with cleanness—cleanliness being a value learned very early in life. But contrary associations can be, and sometimes are, easily built up.

One four-year-old boy was taken by train from Boston to San Francisco. He was enchanted by the friendly Negro porter. For fully two years thereafter he fantasied that he was a porter, and complained bitterly that he was not colored so that he could qualify for the position.

We have discussed the immensely important role of language in building fences for our mental categories and our emotional responses. This factor is so crucial...as it bears on childhood learning.

In Goodman's study it turned out that fully half the nursery school children knew the word "nigger." Few of them understood what the epithet culturally implies. But they knew that the word was potent. It was forbidden, taboo, and always fetched some type of strong response from the teachers. It was therefore a "power word." Not infrequently in a temper tantrum a child would call his teacher (whether white or colored) a "nigger" or a "dirty nigger." The term expressed an emotion—nothing more. Nor did it always express anger—sometimes merely excitement. Children wildly racing around, shrieking at play might, in order to enhance their orgies, yell "nigger, nigger, nigger." As a strong word it seemed fit to vocalize the violent expenditure of energy under way....

Control and Prejudice

To the prejudiced person things seem to happen "out there." He has no control over his destiny. He believes, for example, that "although many people may scoff, it may be shown that astrology can explain a lot of things." Tolerant people, by contrast, tend to believe that our fate lies not in our stars, but in ourselves.

Gordon W. Allport, *The Nature of Prejudice*, 1954.

One little boy was agreeing with his mother, who was warning him never to play with niggers. He said, "No, Mother, I never play with niggers. I only play with white and black children." This child was developing aversion to the term "nigger," without having the slightest idea what the term meant. In other words, the aversion is being set up prior to acquiring a referent....

Children often cry if they are called names. Their self-esteem is wounded by any epithet: naughty, dirty, harum-scarum, nigger, dago, Jap, or what not. To escape this verbal realism of early childhood, they often reassure themselves, when they are a little older, with the self-restorative jingle: Sticks and stones may break my bones, but names can never hurt me. But it takes a few years for them to learn that a name is not a thing-in-itself. Verbal realism may never be fully shaken off. The rigidity of linguistic categories may continue in adult thinking. To some adults "communist" or "Jew" is a dirty word—and a dirty thing—an indissoluble unity, as it may be to a child.

Learning Prejudice: Stage One

Janet, six years of age, was trying hard to integrate her obedience to her mother with her daily social contacts. One day she came running home and asked, "Mother, what is the name of the children I am supposed to hate?"

Janet's wistful question leads us into a theoretical summary of the present chapter.

Janet is stumbling at the threshold of some abstraction. She wishes to form the right category. She intends to oblige her mother by hating the right people when she can find out who they are.

In this situation we suspect the preceding stages in Janet's developmental history:

1. She identifies with the mother, or at least strongly craves the mother's affection and approval. We may imagine that the home is not "permissive" in atmosphere, but somewhat stern and critical. Janet may have found that she must be on her toes to please her parent. Otherwise she will suffer rejection or punishment. In any event, she has developed a habit of obedience.

2. While she has apparently no strong fear of strangers at the present time, she has learned to be circumspect. Experiences of insecurity with people outside the family circle may be a factor in her present effort to define her circle of loyalties.

3. She undoubtedly has gone through the initial period of curiosity and interest in racial and ethnic differences. She knows now that human beings are clustered into groups—that there are important distinctions if only she can identify them. In the case of Negro and white the visibility factor has helped her. But then she discovered that subtler differences were also important; Jews somehow differed from gentiles; wops from Americans; doctors from salesmen. She is now aware of group differences, though not yet clear concerning all the relevant cues.

4. She has encountered the stage of linguistic precedence in learning. In fact, she is now in this stage. She knows that group X (she knows neither its name nor its identity) is somehow hateworthy. She already has the emotional meaning but lacks the referential meaning. She seeks now to integrate the proper content with the

emotion. She wishes to define her category so as to make her future behavior conform to her mother's desires....

As soon as Janet's mother gives a clear answer to Janet, she will in all probability enter a second period of prejudice—one that we may call the period of *total rejection*. Suppose the mother answers, "I told you not to play with Negro children. They are dirty; they have diseases; and they will hurt you. Now don't let me catch you at it." If Janet by now has learned to distinguish Negroes from other groups, even from the dark-skinned Mexican children, or Italians—in other words, if she now has the adult category in mind—she will undoubtedly reject all Negroes, in all circumstances, and with considerable feeling.

The research of Blake and Dennis well illustrates the point. It will be recalled that these investigators studied Southern white children in the fourth and fifth grades (ten- and eleven-year-olds). They asked such questions as, "Which are more musical—Negroes or white people?" "Which are more clean?"—and many questions of a similar type. These children had, by the age of ten, learned to reject the Negro category *totally*. No favorable quality was ascribed to Negroes more often than to whites. In effect, whites had all the virtues; Negroes, none.

Hierarchy and Prejudice

The prejudiced person looks for hierarchy in society. Power arrangements are definite—something he can understand and count on. He likes authority, and says that what America needs is "more discipline." By discipline, of course, he means *outer* discipline, preferring, so to speak, to see people's backbones on the outside rather than on the inside. When students are asked to list the names of great people they most admired, prejudiced students usually gave names of leaders who had exercised power and control over others (Napoleon, Bismark) whereas the unprejudiced listed, more typically, artists, humanitarians, scientists (Lincoln, Einstein).

Gordon W. Allport, *The Nature of Prejudice*, 1954.

While this totalized rejection certainly starts earlier (in many children it will be found by the age of seven or eight), it seems to reach its ethnocentric peak in early puberty. First- and second-grade children often elect to play with, or sit beside, a child of different race or ethnic membership. This friendliness usually disappears in the fifth grade. At that time children choose their own group almost exclusively. Negroes select Negroes, Italians select Italians, and so on.

As children grow older, they normally lose this tendency to total rejection and overgeneralization. Blake and Dennis found that in the 12th grade the white youth ascribed several favorable stereotypes to Negroes. They considered them more musical, more easy-going, better dancers.

Thus, after a period of *total rejection*, a stage of *differentiation* sets in. The prejudices grow less totalized. Escape clauses are written into the attitude in order to make it more rational and more acceptable to the individual. One says, "Some of my best friends are Jews." Or, "I am not prejudiced against Negroes—I always loved my black Mammy." The child who is first learning adult categories of rejection is not able to make such gracious exceptions. It takes him the first six to eight years of his life to learn total rejection, and another six years or so to modify it. The actual adult creed in his culture is complex indeed. It allows for (and in many ways encourages) ethnocentrism. At the same time, one must give lip service to democracy and equality, or at least ascribe some good qualities to the minority group and somehow plausibly justify the remaining disapproval that one expresses. It takes the child well into adolescence to learn the peculiar double-talk appropriate to prejudice in a democracy.

Mastering the Art

Around the age of eight, children often *talk* in a highly prejudiced manner. They have learned their categories and their totalized rejection. But the rejection is chiefly verbal. While they may damn the Jews, the wops, the Catholics, they may still *behave* in a relatively democratic manner. They may play with them even while they talk against them. The "total rejection" is chiefly a verbal matter.

Now when the teaching of the school takes effect, the child learns a new verbal norm: he must talk democractically. He must profess to regard all races and creeds as equal. Hence, by the age of 12, we may find *verbal* acceptance, but *behavioral* rejection. By this age the prejudices have finally affected conduct, even while the verbal, democratic norms are beginning to take effect.

The paradox, then, is that younger children may talk undemocratically, but behave democratically, whereas children in puberty may talk (at least in school) democratically but behave with true prejudice. By the age of 15, considerable skill is shown in imitating the adult pattern. Prejudiced talk and democratic talk are reserved for appropriate occasions, and rationalizations are ready for whatever occasions require them. Even conduct is varied according to circumstances. One may be friendly with a Negro in the kitchen, but hostile to a Negro who comes to the front door. Double-dealing, like double-talk, is hard to learn. It takes the entire period of childhood and much of adolescence to master the art of ethnocentrism.

*"All civilizations derive from the white race...
[and] none can exist without its help."*

The White Race
Is Superior

Joseph Arthur comte de Gobineau

Joseph Arthur comte de Gobineau (1816-1882) was a French diplomat and man of letters. The "Father of Modern Racism," de Gobineau was one of the earliest proponents of the theory of Aryan racial superiority and supremacy. In his major work, *The Inequality of Human Races*, he methodically unveiled the cultural and physical characteristics which separated the three major racial groupings (black, yellow and white). Significantly, he attributed these differences to innately unequal abilities among the races. His conclusion was that the white race in general and the Aryan white in particular were culturally superior to all others. In the following viewpoint, he outlined those features that he believed characterized each race, concluding with the assertion that "all civilizations derive from the white race."

As you read, consider the following questions:

1. According to the author, what are the characteristics of the "black race"?
2. In the author's opinion, how does the "yellow race" differ from the "black race"?
3. In what ways does the author believe the "white race" differs from the other "races"?

Arthur de Gobineau, *The Inequality of Human Races*. New York: G.P. Putnam's Sons, 1915.

I have shown the unique place in the organic world occupied by the human species, the profound physical, as well as moral, differences separating it from all other kinds of living creatures. Considering it by itself, I have been able to distinguish on physiological grounds alone, three great and clearly marked types, the black, the yellow, and the white. However uncertain the aims of physiology may be, however meagre its resources, however defective its methods, it can proceed thus far with absolute certainty.

The Black Race

The negroid variety is the lowest, and stands at the foot of the ladder. The animal character, that appears in the shape of the pelvis, is stamped on the negro from birth, and foreshadows his destiny. His intellect will always move within a very narrow circle. He is not however a mere brute, for behind his low receding brow, in the middle of his skull, we can see signs of a powerful energy, however crude its objects. If his mental faculties are dull or even non-existent, he often has an intensity of desire, and so of will, which may be called terrible. Many of his senses, especially taste and smell, are developed to an extent unknown to the other two races.

The very strength of his sensations is the most striking proof of his inferiority. All food is good in his eyes, nothing disgusts or repels him. What he desires is to eat, to eat furiously, and to excess; no carrion is too revolting to be swallowed by him. It is the same with odours; his inordinate desires are satisfied with all, however coarse or even horrible. To these qualities may be added an instability and capriciousness of feeling, that cannot be tied down to any single object, and which, so far as he is concerned, do away with all distinctions of good and evil. We might even say that the violence with which he pursues the object that has aroused his senses and inflamed his desires is a guarantee of the desires being soon satisfied and the object forgotten. Finally, he is equally careless of his own life and that of others; he kills willingly, for the sake of killing; and this human machine, in whom it is so easy to arouse emotion, shows, in face of suffering, either a monstrous indifference or a cowardice that seeks a voluntary refuge in death.

The Yellow Race

The yellow race is the exact opposite of this type. The skull points forward, not backward. The forehead is wide and bony, often high and projecting. The shape of the face is triangular, the nose and chin showing none of the coarse protuberances that mark the negro. There is further a general proneness to obesity, which, though not confined to the yellow type, is found there more frequently than in the others. The yellow man has little physical energy, and is inclined to apathy; he commits none of the strange excesses so common among negroes. His desires are feeble, his will-power rather obstinate than violent; his longing for material pleasures, though constant, is kept within bounds. A rare glutton by nature, he shows far more discrimination in his choice of food. He tends to mediocrity in everything; he understands easily enough anything not too deep or sublime. He has a love of utility and a respect for order, and knows the value of a certain amount of freedom. He is practical, in the narrowest sense of the word. He does not dream or theorize; he invents little, but can appreciate and take over what is useful to him. His whole desire is to live in the easiest and most comfortable way possible. The yellow races are thus clearly superior to the black. Every founder of a civilization would wish the backbone of his society, his middle class, to consist of such men. But no civilized society could be created by them; they could not supply its nerve-force, or set in motion the springs of beauty and action.

Nordic Superiority

Talking with the aid of hands and feet is characteristic of non-Nordics, whereas the Nordic man stands calmly, often enough with his hands in his pockets.

Generally speaking, the Nordic race alone can emit sounds of untroubled clearness, whereas among non-Nordics the pronunciation is impure, the individual sounds are more confused and like the noises made by animals, such as barking, sniffing, snoring, squeaking....

If non-Nordics are more closely allied to monkeys and apes than to Nordics, why is it possible for them to mate with Nordics and not with apes? The answer is this: it has not been proved that non-Nordics cannot mate with apes.

Hermann Gauch, *New Bases of Racial Research.*

We come now to the white peoples. These are gifted with reflective energy, or rather with an energetic intelligence. They have a feeling for utility, but in a sense far wider and higher, more courageous and ideal, than the yellow races; a perseverance that takes account of obstacles and ultimately finds a means of overcoming them; a greater physical power, an extraordinary instinct for order, not merely as a guarantee of peace and tranquillity, but as an indispensable means of self-preservation. At the same time, they have a remarkable, and even extreme, love of liberty, and are openly hostile to the formalism under which the Chinese are glad to vegetate, as well as to the strict despotism which is the only way of governing the negro.

The white races are, further, distinguished by an extraordinary attachment to life. They know better how to use it, and so, as it would seem, set a greater price on it; both in their own persons and those of others, they are more sparing of life. When they are cruel, they are conscious of their cruelty; it is very doubtful whether such a consciousness exists in the negro. At the same time, they have discovered reasons why they should surrender this busy life of theirs, that is so precious to them. The principal motive is honour, which under various names has played an enormous part in the ideas of the race from the beginning. I need hardly add that the word honour, together with all the civilizing influences connoted by it, is unknown to both the yellow and the black man....

The White Race

Such is the lesson of history. It shows us that all civilizations derive from the white race, that none can exist without its help, and that a society is great and brilliant only so far as it preserves the blood of the noble group that created it, provided that this group itself belongs to the most illustrious branch of our species.

"Exclude [the Aryan]—and...darkness will again descend on the earth, human culture will pass, and the world turn to a desert."

The Aryan Race Is Superior

Adolf Hitler

The name of Adolf Hitler has become synonomous with racism in its most vile form. His notions of Aryan racial superiority and his hatred of Jews, while derived from earlier writers such as Arthur de Gobineau and Houston Stewart Chamberlain, were carried to new and vitriolic extremes. Unlike most racists of similar opinion, Hitler, as chancellor of Germany from 1933 to 1945, was able to translate his ideas into deeds. The result was the annihilation of tens of millions of human lives during World War II. Hitler's peculiar brand of racism was unequivocally articulated in *Mein Kampf*, a book that became the bible of the Nazi movement in Germany. In the following viewpoint, excerpted from *Mein Kampf*, Hitler attempts to explain how and why the Aryan peoples are the progenitors of human culture.

As you read, consider the following questions:

1. According to the author, what role do "lower human beings" play in helping Aryans further human culture?
2. What does the author claim happens when those peoples subjected by the Aryans begin "to raise themselves up"?

It is idle to argue which race or races were the original represent-ative of human culture and hence the real founders of all that we sum up under the word "humanity." It is simpler to raise this ques-tion with regard to the present, and here an easy, clear answer results. All the human culture, all the results of art, science, and technology that we see before us today, are almost exclusively the creative product of the Aryan. This very fact admits of the not un-founded inference that he alone was the founder of all higher humanity, therefore representing the prototype of all that we understand by the word "man." He is the Prometheus of mankind from whose bright forehead the divine spark of genius has sprung at all times, forever kindling anew that fire of knowledge which illumined the night of silent mysteries and thus caused man to climb the path to mastery over the other beings of this earth. Ex-clude him—and perhaps after a few thousand years darkness will again descend on the earth, human culture will pass, and the world turn to a desert.

If we were to divide mankind into three groups, the founders of culture, the bearers of culture, the destroyers of culture, only the Aryan could be considered as the representative of the first group. From him originate the foundations and walls of all human crea-tion, and only the outward form and color are determined by the changing traits of character of the various peoples. He provides the mightiest building stones and plans for all human progress and only the execution corresponds to the nature of the varying men and races....

Bearers of Culture

Creatively active peoples always have a fundamental creative gift, even if it should not be recognizable to the eyes of superficial observers. Here, too, outward recognition is possible only in con-sequence of accomplished deeds, since the rest of the world is not capable of recognizing genius in itself, but sees only its visible manifestations in the form of inventions, discoveries, buildings, pictures, etc.; here again it often takes a long time before the world can fight its way through to this knowledge. Just as in the life of the outstanding individual, genius or extraordinary ability strives for practical realization only when spurred on by special occasions, likewise in the life of nations the creative forces and capacities which are present can often be exploited only when definite preconditions invite.

We see this most distinctly in connection with the race which has been and is the bearer of human cultural development—the Aryans. As soon as Fate leads them toward special conditions, their latent abilities begin to develop in a more and more rapid sequence and to mold themselves into tangible forms. The cultures which they found in such cases are nearly always decisively determined by the existing soil, the given climate, and—the subjected people.

212

This last item, to be sure, is almost the most decisive. The more primitive the technical foundations for a cultural activity, the more necessary is the presence of human helpers who, organizationally assembled and employed, must replace the force of the machine. Without this possibility of using lower human beings, the Aryan would never have been able to take his first steps toward his future culture; just as without the help of various suitable beasts which he knew how to tame, he would not have arrived at a technology which is now gradually permitting him to do without these beasts. The saying, "The Moor has worked off his debt, the Moor can go," unfortunately has only too deep a meaning. For thousands of years the horse had to serve man and help him lay the foundations of a development which now, in consequence of the motor car, is making the horse superfluous. In a few years his activity will have ceased, but without his previous collaboration man might have had a hard time getting where he is today.

Lower Human Types

Thus, for the formation of higher cultures the existence of lower human types was one of the most essential preconditions, since they alone were able to compensate for the lack of technical aids without which a higher development is not conceivable. It is certain that the first culture of humanity was based less on the tamed animal than on the use of lower human beings....

Preserving Racial Purity

Imbued with the knowledge that the purity of German blood is the necessary prerequisite for the existence of the German nation, and inspired by an inflexible will to maintain the existence of the German nation for all future times, the Reichstag has unanimously adopted the following law, which is now proclaimed:

ARTICLE 1. (1) Any marriage between Jews and citizens of German or kindred blood are herewith forbidden. Marriages entered into despite this law are invalid, even if they are arranged abroad as a means of circumventing this law.

The Nuremberg Laws on Citizenship and Race, September/November, 1935.

The progress of humanity is like climbing an endless ladder; it is impossible to climb higher without first taking the lower steps. Thus, the Aryan had to take the road to which reality directed him and not the one that would appeal to the imagination of a modern pacifist. The road of reality is hard and difficult, but in the end it leads where our friend would like to bring humanity by dreaming, but unfortunately removes more than bringing it closer.

Hence it is no accident that the first cultures arose in places where the Aryan, in his encounters with lower peoples, subjugated them and bent them to his will. They then became the first technical instrument in the service of a developing culture.

Thus, the road which the Aryan had to take was clearly marked out. As a conqueror he subjected the lower beings and regulated their practical activity under his command, according to his will and for his aims. But in directing them to a useful, though arduous activity, he not only spared the life of those he subjected; perhaps he gave them a fate that was better than their previous so-called "freedom." As long as he ruthlessly upheld the master attitude, not only did he really remain master, but also the preserver and increaser of culture. For culture was based exclusively on his abilities and hence on his actual survival. As soon as the subjected people began to raise themselves up and probably approached the conqueror in language, the sharp dividing wall between master and servant fell. The Aryan gave up the purity of his blood and, therefore, lost his sojourn in the paradise which he had made for himself. He became submerged in the racial mixture, and gradually, more and more, lost his cultural capacity, until at last, not only mentally but also physically, he began to resemble the subjected aborigines more than his own ancestors. For a time he could live on the existing cultural benefits, but then petrifaction set in and he fell a prey to oblivion.

Loss of Pure Blood

Thus cultures and empires collapsed to make place for new formations.

Blood mixture and the resultant drop in the racial level is the sole cause of the dying out of old cultures; for men do not perish as a result of lost wars, but by the loss of that force of resistance which is contained only in pure blood.

All who are not of good race in this world are chaff.

And all occurrences in world history are only the expression of the races' instinct of self-preservation, in the good or bad sense.

"The white race had six thousand...years in which to destroy the truth and to destroy the Aboriginal Black People who were created in truth."

The Black Race Is Superior

Elijah Muhammad

Elijah Muhammad was the founder of the Black Muslim religion. According to the Black Muslims, Allah (God) appeared in America in July 1930 in the person of Master Fard Muhammad to appoint the Honorable Elijah Muhammad his final messenger and prophet. During his mission, Mr. Muhammad preached racial separation and black supremacy, claiming that blacks are morally superior while whites are evil and motivated by the devil. He died on February 25, 1975. As a religious organization, the Black Muslims are still active throughout the United States. The controversial Minister Louis Farrakhan is currently the Muslims' most vocal spokesperson. The following viewpoint is taken from *Muhammad Speaks*, a weekly Muslim publication that typically featured articles by Elijah Muhammad. In it, Mr. Muhammad offers his explanation for the presence of confusion and evil in the world.

As you read, consider the following questions:

1. According to the author, who is Yakub and what did he do?
2. To what does the author attribute the confusion which reigns in the world?

Elijah Muhammad, "Confusion," *Muhammad Speaks*, September 28, 1973.

In the stage of the making of the devil (white race) confusion existed between the Arab world and Yakub (father of the devil).

Yakub's (a Black scientist) teachings to his made-man (white race) was that they make mischief in the land, and rule the Aboriginal Black People, by dividing them one against the other.

In order to destroy the power of the enemy (white race) at that time, they decided to drive Yakub's made-man (white race) into the hills and mountains of west Asia (which is now known as Europe). Six thousand (6,000) years ago that desolate wilderness was known as west Asia.

Disagreement was accepted, therefore the devil had to be driven into what is now called Europe.

According to the teachings of God, Who Came in the Person of Master Fard Muhammad, to me: EU stands for hillside and ROPE means that these people (white race) were roped in and isolated from the peaceful world of the Muslim Arabs.

After Yakub's made-man (white race) was driven out, the Arabs were not completely at peace because the devil had left his stain of dissatisfaction and mischief-making among the people of the Arab world. The stain remained because it was due to the given time of Yakub's made-man to serve the people with that which they never were served under before (confusion and bloodshed).

The Arabs thought that isolation, and the banishing of the white race into the hills and cavesides of Europe would be the end of Yakub's made-man (white race).

Yakub's Law

The white man was made by nature to do that which his father made him for. He could not help but carry out the law under which he was made. And he has been doing so ever since he was made. He has not disobeyed his father, Yakub's Law.

The reader will agree with me, that this is perfectly true. The white man divides the so-called Negro (Aboriginal Black People) until, today you can hardly unite two so-called Negroes together. He divided the people by telling other than the truth and teaching it to the world.

All of this causes confusion—anything opposite to the truth. The truth will finally have to go to war against other than the truth, in order to keep truth, and the light of the truth, shining in the heart of those who love truth.

Confusion, revolution—this trouble and warring is due to the fact that it is time that the truth should reign, and the Great God of Truth, Master Fard Muhammad, To Whom Praises are due forever is in Person today, to see that truth triumphs over falsehood. And the lovers of falsehood will fight to the bitter end to oppose truth and prevent truth from triumphing over the nations of the earth.

There are so many of our Black People who have been reared under falsehood, that they will join the forces of falsehood to try to prevent truth from being the victor. This is an evil world that we are now living in. It has become the bursting point of its world. "As she has done so shall it be done unto her."

She has divided the nations and has put brothers fighting against brothers. Now she must be divided and her brother of evil put to fighting with her. This is going on at the present time.

Muhammad Speaks, July 13, 1973.

When we learn the cause of the ugly situation of the world, we can see just why it should be like it is. Corruption of evil is poured upon all of the living of the earth. It is no easy thing to restore the nation of righteous back into righteousness, after being ruled under other than right, for six thousand (6,000) years. Just one thousand (1,000) years is a long, long time.

But, the white race had six thousand (6,000) years in which to destroy the truth and to destroy the Aboriginal Black People who were created in truth.

The Trouble-Makers

Now to separate them and to put them back again into their own spheres, and remove the trouble-makers. The trouble-makers (white race) cannot have a place anywhere on the earth because the white race has covered the earth of the Aboriginal Black People. There is nowhere to hide him as there was six thousand (6,000) years ago when he was driven into the hills and cavesides of Europe.

Every square foot of civilization today is under the rule of the trouble-makers. Therefore, it will not do us any good to exile him to rid ourselves of this mighty and powerful enemy, so Allah (God) Has Decided, this time to burn the worse one of them, and destroy the power of those that are not burned.

The book of Daniel, in the Bible, has the clear answer to the confusion and the trouble-maker. He singles out one beast (as they are called) and prophesies that they would be taken and killed outright. This prophecy corresponds with the prophecy in the Book of Revelation, in the Bible, "that one beast (4th beast) was killed outright and his body given to the burning flame."

Daniel and the Revelation of John shows the same end of Yakub's made-man. This knowledge is not new to the white man. The white man has known this all of his life. But, what is new in this is that my Black People never knew the 'theology side' of the Bible. They have only used guessing. Therefore, they have misled their, and our, own Black People, spiritually.

The right way out for them now, and the truth that will establish them again on the earth as a nation, is to accept their own. But it is hard for them to believe; therefore, God Himself Will Have to Resort to punishment, for them, in order to get them to believe.

Confused Americans

The confused Americans and the confused government cannot be helped, because it is God Himself Who Is Causing their confusion. They confuse all with whom they come into contact.

The white man's greatest effort to rule us was to divide one against the other. He divided Korea, as you know, with one brother against the other. He divided China, with one brother against the other. There out in Formosa he has a brother of China, sitting there to fight his brother China, on the mainland. He divided Viet Nam just like he did Korea. Then he made the two brothers fight and kill each other while he (white man) acted as judge.

This is what Yakub taught him. "Divide them and let them fight. When they are fighting with each other, you step in and tell them to let you judge their affair and when they allow you (white man) to judge their affair then you can rule them both."

The Murderer

So all of this is now coming to an end, for the God of Heaven Has Ordered it. Look at the opposition and prosecution to kill you because you believe in the truth. They do not care how they kill you, just as long as you are dead. They shoot you in the back. They shoot you while you lay asleep. They shoot you anywhere. They hide behind a bush and shoot you. The white man is a murderer by nature. Jesus did not miss it in the Bible, John 8:44 "...He was a murderer from the beginning, and abode not in the truth...for his is a liar..." His father made him under this.

So when you hear me say that I cannot blame the made-man (white man) for this is what he was by nature to do, that does not mean that you, WE will endure with the white man forever, just because, by nature he is evil. The real blame is on Yakub who made the devil (white race).

Confusion, confusion and revolution. Everybody is opposed to the other. Twenty-four hours a day America is broadcasting her confusion. Only a few, here and there, among the white race, desire to see truth and justice reign instead of confusion, murder and injustice.

Universal confusion and revolution. I thank you.

"Genetic differences are of little significance in determining the social and cultural differences between different groups of men."

No Race
Is Superior

United Nations Educational, Scientific and Cultural Organization

On June 8, 1951, an international group of physical anthropologists and geneticists drafted a text whose subject was the nature of race and racial differences. Sponsored by the United Nations Educational, Scientific and Cultural Organization (UNESCO), the purpose of the statement was to offer the authoritative offices of the United Nations in the worldwide fight against racism. The succinct statement is still widely recognized as a durable and valid argument disavowing the concept of inferiority based upon physical differences among humans. The following viewpoint offers the complete text of the 1951 UNESCO statement on race.

As you read, consider the following questions:

1. How does the author explain hereditary differences among populations?
2. Why do anthropologists exclude mental characteristics in their classification of human races?
3. According to the author, what accounts for the differing psychological attributes of national groups?

United Nations Educational, Scientific and Cultural Organization, *The Race Concept: Results of an Inquiry.* Published by UNESCO, Paris, 1951.

1. Scientists are generally agreed that all men living today belong to a single species, *Homo sapiens*, and are derived from a common stock, even though there is some dispute as to when and how different human groups diverged from this common stock.

The concept of race is unanimously regarded by anthropologists as a classificatory device providing a zoological frame within which the various groups of mankind may be arranged and by means of which studies of evolutionary processes can be facilitated. In its anthropological sense, the world "race" should be reserved for groups of mankind possessing well-developed and primarily heritable physical differences from other groups. Many populations can be so classified but, because of the complexity of human history, there are also many populations which cannot easily be fitted into a racial classification.

Hereditary Differences

2. Some of the physical differences between human groups are due to differences in hereditary constitution and some to differences in the environments in which they have been brought up. In most cases, both influences have been at work. The science of genetics suggests that the hereditary differences among populations of a single species are the results of the action of two sets of processes. On the one hand, the genetic composition of isolated populations is constantly but gradually being altered by natural selection and by occasional changes (mutations) in the material particles (genes) which control heredity. Populations are also affected by fortuitous changes in gene frequency and by marriage customs. On the other hand, crossing is constantly breaking down the differentiations so set up. The new mixed populations, in so far as they, in turn, become isolated, are subject to the same processes, and these may lead to further changes. Existing races are merely the result, considered at a particular moment in time, of the total effect of such processes on the human species. The hereditary characters to be used in the classification of human groups, the limits of their variation within these groups, and thus the extent of the classificatory subdivisions adopted may legitimately differ according to the scientific purpose in view.

Culture and Race

3. National, religious, geographical, linguistic and cultural groups do not necessarily coincide with racial groups; and the cultural traits of such groups have no demonstrated connexion with racial traits. Americans are not a race, nor are Frenchmen, nor Germans; nor *ipso facto* is any other national group. Moslems and Jews are no more races than are Roman Catholics and Protestants; nor are people who live in Iceland or Britain or India, or who speak English or any other language, or who are culturally Turkish or Chinese and the like, thereby describable as races. The

221

use of the term "race" in speaking of such groups may be a serious error, but it is one which is habitually committed.

4. Human races can be, and have been, classified in different ways by different anthropologists. Most of them agree in classifying the greater part of existing mankind into at least three large units, which may be called major groups (in French *grand-races*, in German *Hauptrassen*). Such a classification does not depend on any single physical character, nor does, for example, skin colour by itself necessarily distinguish one major group from another. Furthermore, so far as it has been possible to analyse them, the differences in physical structure which distinguish one major group from another give no support to popular notions of any general "superiority" or "inferiority" which are sometimes implied in referring to these groups.

Overlap of Characteristics

Broadly speaking, individuals belonging to different major groups of mankind are distinguishable by virtue of their physical characters, but individual members, or small groups, belonging to different races within the same major group are usually not so distinguishable. Even the major groups grade into each other, and the physical traits by which they and the races within them are characterized overlap considerably. With respect to most, if not all, measurable characters, the differences among individuals belonging to the same race are greater than the differences that occur between the observed averages for two or more races within the same major group.

All Are Equal

In the realm of culture there is enough room to accommodate the diversified contributions not only of different individuals but also of every nation and race. It is a waste of time to discuss which particular contributions are superior and which inferior. There is no common measure applicable to the works of a poet, an artist, a philosopher, a scientist, and the simple kindness of heart of a plain man. Humanity needs them all.

L.C. Dunn and Theodosius Dobzhansky, *Heredity, Race and Society,* 1952.

5. Most anthropologists do not include mental characteristics in their classification of human races. Studies within a single race have shown that both innate capacity and environmental opportunity determine the results of tests of intelligence and temperament, though their relative importance is disputed.

When intelligence tests, even non-verbal, are made on a group of non-literate people, their scores are usually lower than those of more civilized people. It has been recorded that different groups of the same race occupying similarly high levels of civilization may yield considerable differences in intelligence tests. When, however, the two groups have been brought up from childhood in similar environments, the differences are usually very slight. Moreover, there is good evidence that, given similar opportunities, the average performance (that is to say, the performance of the individual who is representative because he is surpassed by as many as he surpasses), and the variation round it, do not differ appreciably from one race to another.

Even those psychologists who claim to have found the greatest differences in intelligence between groups of different racial origin, and have contended that they are hereditary, always report that some members of the group of inferior performance surpass not merely the lowest ranking member of the superior group, but also the average of its members. In any case, it has never been possible to separate members of two groups on the basis of mental capacity, as they can often be separated on a basis of religion, skin colour, hair form or language. It is possible, though not proved, that some types of innate capacity for intellectual and emotional responses are commoner in one human group than in another, but it is certain that, within a single group, innate capacities vary as much as, if not more than, they do between different groups.

Mental Defects

The study of the heredity of psychological characteristics is beset with difficulties. We know that certain mental diseases and defects are transmitted from one generation to the next, but we are less familiar with the part played by heredity in the mental life of normal individuals. The normal individual, irrespective of race, is essentially educable. It follows that his intellectual and moral life is largely conditioned by his training and by his physical and social environment.

It often happens that a national group may appear to be characterized by particualr psychological attributes. The superficial view would be that this is due to race. Scientifically, however, we realize that any common psychological attribute is more likely to be due to a common historical and social background, and that such attributes may obscure the fact that, within different populations consisting of many human types, one will find approximately the same range of temperament and intelligence.

6. The scientific material available to us at present does not justify the conclusion that inherited genetic differences are a major factor in producing the differences between the cultures and cultural achievements of different peoples or groups. It does indicate, on the contrary, that a major factor is explaining such differences in the cultural experience which each group has undergone.

7. There is no evidence for the existence of so-called "pure" races. Skeletal remains provide the basis of our limited knowledge about earlier races. In regard to race mixture, the evidence points to the fact that human hybridization has been going on for an indefininte but considerable time. Indeed, one of the processes of race formation and race extinction or absorption is by means of hybridization between races. As there is no reliable evidence that disadvantageous effects are produced thereby, no biological justification exists for prohibiting intermarriage between persons of different races.

8. We now have to consider the bearing of these statements on the problem of human equality. We wish to emphasize that equality of opportunity and equality in law in no way depend, as ethical principles, upon the assertion that human beings are in fact equal in endowment.

In Summary

9. We have thought it worth while to set out in a formal manner what is at present scientifically established concerning individual and group differences.

(a) In matters of race, the only characteristics which anthropologist have so far been able to use effectively as a basis for classification are physical (anatomical and physiological).

(b) Available scientific knowledge provides no basis for believing that the groups of mankind differ in their innate capacity for intellectual and emotional development.

(c) Some biological differences between human beings within a single race may be as great as, or greater than, the same biological differences between races.

(d) Vast social changes have occurred that have not been connected in any with with changes in racial type. Historical and sociological studies thus support the view that genetic differences are of little significance in determining the social and cultural differences between different groups of men.

(e) There is no evidence that race mixture produces disadvantageous results from a biological point of view. The social results of race mixture, whether for good or ill, can generally be traced to social factors.

Recognizing Statements That Are Provable

From various sources of information we are constantly confronted with statements and generalizations about social and moral problems. In order to think clearly about these problems, it is useful to be able to make a basic distinction between statements for which evidence can be found and other statements which cannot be verified or proved because evidence is not available or the issue is too controversial.

Readers should constantly be aware that magazines, newspapers, or other sources often contain statements of a controversial or questionable nature. The following activity is designed to allow experimentation with statements that can be proved or disproved and those that cannot.

Most of the following statements are taken from the viewpoints in this chapter. Consider each statement carefully. *Mark P for any statement you believe is provable; that is, evidence could be found which clearly shows the statement to be true or false. Mark U for any statement you feel is unprovable; that is, it cannot be proven to be true or false—it is merely an opinion. Mark C for any statement you think is too controversial to be proved to everyone's satisfaction; that is, there is evidence on both sides and it cannot definitely be shown to be true or false.*

If you are doing this activity as a member of a class or group, compare your answers with those of other class or group members. Be able to defend your answers. You may discover that others will come to different conclusions than you. Listening to the reasons others present for their answers may give you valuable insights in recognizing statements that are provable.

If you are reading this book alone, ask others if they agree with your answers. You too will find this interaction very valuable.

P = *provable*
U = *unprovable*
C = *too controversial*

1. Children raised in a home that is suppressive, harsh, or critical—where the parents' word is law—are more likely to be prejudiced.

2. The first civilized humans relied less on the tamed animal than on the use of lower human beings.

3. The differences in physical appearance which distinguish one major racial group from another do not support the popular notions of any general "superiority" or "inferiority" among races.

4. All civilizations derive from the white race.

5. The confused American and the confused government cannot be helped, because it is God himself who is causing their confusion.

6. All humans living today belong to a single species, *Homo sapiens*, and are derived from a common stock.

7. The white man is a murderer by nature, which Jesus said in the Bible, John 8:44: "He was a murderer from the beginning and abode not in the truth."

8. The black man is equally careless of his own life and that of others; he kills willingly, for the sake of killing.

9. Children form their social attitudes and prejudices by the time they are six years old.

10. When the Aryan conquered and subjected the lower peoples, he not only directed them toward a useful, though arduous activity, he also gave them a fate that was better than their previous so-called "freedom."

11. By age fifteen, children imitate the adult pattern of talking democratically but behaving with true prejudice, while at age eight, children talk undemocratically but behave democratically toward other children.

12. The physical characteristics of the negro reflect his animal nature and determine his destiny.

13. Intermarriage between races is the sole cause of the death of old cultures; for men do not perish because they lose wars, but because they lose the force of resistance that is contained only in pure blood.

14. So called "pure" races do not exist.

15. Americans are not a race, nor are the French nor Germans; Moslems and Jews are no more races than are Roman Catholics or Protestants.

Bibliography

The following list of books and periodicals deals with the subject matter of this chapter.

Theodor W. Adorno et al.	*The Authoritarian Personality.* New York: Harper and Row, 1950.
Anti-Defamation League of B'nai B'rith	*Extremism on the Right.* New York: The Anti-Defamation League of B'nai B'rith, 1983.
Houston Stewart Chamberlain	*Foundations of the Nineteenth Century.* London: Bodley Head Ltd., 1912.
Carlton S. Coon	*The Races of Europe.* New York: The Macmillan Company, 1939.
Stephen Jay Gould	"Human Equality Is a Contingent Fact of History," *Natural History,* November 1984.
Madison Grant	*The Passing of the Great Race.* New York: Charles Scribner's Sons, 1916.
Phyllis Katz, ed.	*Towards the Elimination of Racism.* New York: Pergamon Press, 1976.
C. Eric Lincoln	*The Black Muslims in America.* Boston: Beacon Press, 1973.
Gary T. Marx	*Protest and Prejudice.* New York: Harper and Row, 1967.
Ashley Montagu	*Man's Most Dangerous Myth.* New York: Harper and Brothers, 1952.
National Review	"Hitler Knew Something," September 6, 1985.
Charles Patterson	*Anti-Semitism: The Road to the Holocaust and Beyond.* New York: Walker and Company, 1982.
Thomas F. Pettigrew et al.	*Prejudice.* London: The Belknap Press, 1982.
Thomas F. Pettigrew, ed.	*Racial Discrimination in the United States.* New York: New York Free Press, 1975.
Wilmot Robertson	*The Dispossessed Majority.* Cape Canaveral, FL: H. Allen, 1976.
John Williams and J. Kenneth Morland	*Race, Color, and the Young Child.* Chapel Hill, NC: University of North Carolina Press, 1976.

Index

230